IS IT SACRIFICE?

Bill and Shirley Lees

Inter-Varsity Press

OMF Books, Singapore
STL Books, Bromley, Kent

Inter-Varsity Press
38 De Montfort Street, Leicester LE1 7GP, England

Unless otherwise stated, quotations from the Bible are taken from the HOLY BIBLE: NEW INTERNATIONAL VERSION. Copyright © 1978 by the International Bible Society, New York. Published in Great Britain by Hodder and Stoughton Limited, and used by permission of Zondervan Bible Publishers, Grand Rapids, Michigan.

First published 1987

British Library Cataloguing in Publication Data

Lees, Bill
    Is it sacrifice?
    1. Missions—Malaysia, East
    I. Title   II. Lees, Shirley
    266'.0092'2   BV3370.N6

IVP ISBN 0-85110-487-8
OMF ISBN 9971-972-53-0
STL ISBN 1-85078-019-6

Set in Baskerville 11/12 point.
Typeset in Great Britain by TJB Photosetting Ltd., South Witham, Lincolnshire
Printed in Great Britain by Cox & Wyman Ltd, Reading

Inter-Varsity Press is the publishing division of the Universities and Colleges Christian Fellowship (formerly the Inter-Varsity Fellowship), a student movement linking Christian Unions in universities and colleges throughout the United Kingdom and the Republic of Ireland, and a member movement of the International Fellowship of Evangelical Students. For information about local and national activities write to UCCF, 38 De Montfort Street, Leicester LE1 7GP.

OMF Books are published by Overseas Missionary Fellowship, Singapore.

STL Books are published by Send The Light (Operation Mobilisation), PO Box 48, Bromley, Kent, England.

Contents

To all those who prayed for us
and to God
who more than answered prayer

Preface

This is not the sort of book anyone would choose to write. We were asked to share some of the things we learnt from our time in East Malaysia, where we worked with the Borneo Evangelical Mission (now merged with the Overseas Missionary Fellowship). We spent fourteen years there, mostly amongst the Tagal people of Sabah but also had assignments in Sarawak. Sabah and Sarawak, now known as East Malaysia, were British colonies for most of our time there and they form part of the large island of Borneo.

As we have digested some of the lessons over many years, we realize that the learning process has been very varied. Sometimes it has been through what happened to us, sometimes from what we observed, sometimes through studying certain parts of Scripture again and again over a long period of time and against a varying backcloth of experience. Sometimes it has been through success and sometimes through failure and mistakes. We have therefore not attempted artificially to unify the presentation from chapter to chapter.

This is very much a joint project but it would have been difficult to relate everything in the first person plural! I have therefore done the actual writing but, even where not specifically acknowledged, many of the thoughts and insights are Bill's. Others have been worked out mutually as we have shared our lives, our thoughts, the lessons learnt and situations experienced.

We hope you will forgive us that, inevitably, we figure prominently in the story. We hope we have told it in such a way that your eyes will be turned away from us and our experiences to God, who delights to draw his people into partnership with himself, and who seems to be as concerned for our growth and development as he is for the work he shares with us.

SHIRLEY LEES

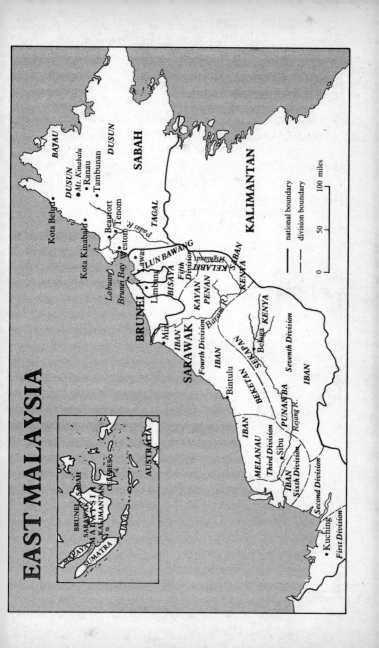

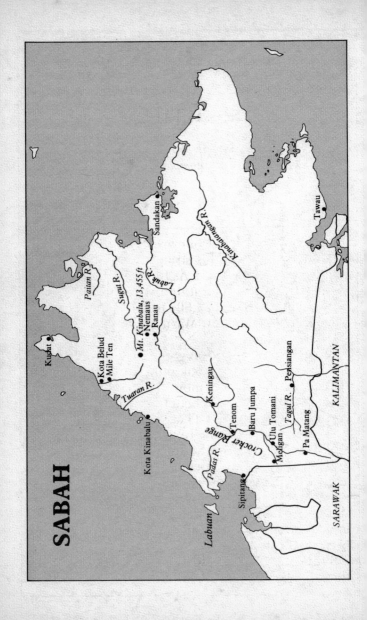

SABAH

1

Is it sacrifice?

Unaccustomed to miracles ● *Living sacrifices* ● *God and company*

'I felt I had to kill that white man. He was disturbing our way of life with his strange talk. So I put my hand on my jungle knife. As I tried to draw it out of its sheath, I couldn't lift it. It was too heavy.'

The congregation of 1,500 tribal people in Sabah were listening intently. Warming to his story, the speaker went on.

'I tried again. It was no good. I couldn't lift it. So I warned everyone. "Look out," I said, "the spirit defending this man is more powerful than all the spirits we know. We had better listen to him." '

And listen they did. That white man was Bill. I well remember when he returned from that visit to a fairly remote part of the area where we were working amongst the Tagal people. He had been amazed at their openness and responsiveness. They were animists, normally in the absolute grip of fear of evil spirits to whom they bowed at all times in total submission. Yet they were all asking how they could become Christians.

'Praise the Lord, we did listen,' this Tagal man continued. 'We are so glad to have Gisar and Rangai [our Bornean names] here with us today. I thank God that he prevented me from killing his servant whom he had sent to bring us his Word.'

Twenty-eight years after God had saved Bill's life, we heard this testimony from a deacon in the now well-established Tagal church of inland Sabah, in East Malaysia. We had been invited back to speak at a number of Easter conventions in 1984, and it was at one of these that this unusually tall and burly Tagal gave us such a warm welcome. He explained how he had been standing just behind Bill while he was surrounded by Tagals. For someone brought up in the jungle, a member of a tribe known in earlier years for its skill in head-hunting, all that was needed was a quick, deft stroke with his jungle knife. But for God's intervention, it is certain that Bill would have died for the sake of the gospel.

Why did God intervene and why did he allow us to wait twenty-eight years to hear about it?

Unaccustomed to miracles

We were not very well adjusted to miracles when we first left England just before Christmas in 1951. True, we had to pray for healing for me shortly after our arrival in Australia en route to Borneo (now East Malaysia). I had arrived and gone straight to bed. Then for the next few weeks, while Bill did a GP locum, and he and doctor friends in Melbourne tried everything they knew, I struggled to stay on my feet. It was clear that, although I was not seriously ill, I was certainly not well enough to do the exacting Wycliffe course (now the Summer Institute of Linguistics). And that was the main reason we had left

England when we did, travelling 12,000 miles to Australia rather than going straight to Borneo.

It seemed unthinkable that God would have taken us all that way and then allowed me to be too unwell to benefit from the course. We prayed in total inexperience and desperation and with little practical faith. However, we had a firm belief in the power and love of God. He graciously answered our prayer.

We were full of praise and thanks – and some amazement! Nevertheless this manifestation of God's care did not stimulate an expectation of the sort of miracles that were needed to demonstrate to the Tagals that Jesus is stronger than Satan.

For centuries, the Tagals had lived in continual fear and daily appeasement of the evil spirits. Omens, through which the spirits communicated, had to be obeyed, whether it meant starvation through neglect of their farms, poverty through frequent animal sacrifices, or ill-health amongst the women and children due to the many taboos and practices connected with childbirth. Disobedience might mean death.

God had opened the way into Tagal country through Amat, a pastor from the neighbouring former head-hunting enemies of the Tagals, the Lun Bawang tribe. He had gone to a village on the fringe of Tagal country some eighteen months ahead of us. He was prepared to pray for miracles.

'If your God is so powerful, ask him to heal my leg,' was the first challenge thrown out to him by a man with a paralysed leg.

'You repent of your sin and I'll pray,' Amat calmly replied.

The man had understood what Amat had been

preaching and teaching. He repented of his submission to Satan and turned to submit to the Lordship of Christ. Amat prayed and the paralysed leg was healed. News of this spread and the next man to ask for prayer was blind. He had to be led around holding on to the end of a stick – it's impossible to lead anyone by the arm or hand along the narrow jungle tracks where everyone walks in single file.

Amat was telling the story of the man born blind.

'Ask your Jesus to give me my sight back,' the blind man called out.

'You repent first,' Amat insisted, and he explained the gospel yet again.

After some days the man said he really believed and wanted to repent. They prayed together, and then Amat prayed for the man's sight to be restored. Later on we actually taught this man to read.

It didn't surprise us that God answered Amat's prayers in this way. He was a fairly new Christian himself. He had seen the miraculous way in which God had dealt with his own people, transforming them from a dying-out community of alcoholics to become a progressive Christian tribe. His faith was simple and direct. The Tagals, who were constantly aware of the supernatural powers of evil spirits, needed to see God's power demonstrated. But we had been brought up in the sophisticated West and we did not have faith to pray that way. Healing of 'nuisance' ailments was one thing, but a paralysed leg and blindness – those things only happened in New Testament times. So God organized a miracle with which we could not interfere and, perhaps partly to keep us from pride, he waited until we had learnt many lessons before he let us hear about it!

Living sacrifices

God used this miracle to extend the break into a stronghold of Satan. He saved Bill's life. He did not ask of us that particular sacrifice. But others of our friends did give their lives. The privations of internment camp took the life of the missionary through whom Amat had come to know the Lord. Two of our post-war missionary colleagues lost their little five-year-old boy. He drowned in the river which runs close to the Bible School (you have to live by a river otherwise there is no water). That river had also taken the life of the head student's little boy some years before (just after we had arrived in Borneo). God had used that tragedy to trigger off a major re-awakening of the church. Later, a young man only a year out from England went to pioneer an area amongst the resistant Iban people and he died through an accident in his first week there. He left a widow, expecting their first child.

There have been other sacrifices too. Sickness — directly caused by living in extremely primitive situations and exposure to tropical diseases. Privations — it was not unusual for one and another of our missionary team, or of the larger team of local pastors, not to know where their next meal was coming from. There were misunderstandings and loneliness. There was oppression from the Evil One.

We are told to present our lives as 'living sacrifices' (Romans 12:1), and that is what we all did, willingly but not without struggles. We ourselves were sure that God had called us to Borneo and were very aware of the privilege of going to a place where God was so obviously in business. It was exciting, but nevertheless we were all too aware of giving up home, good jobs, friends, comfort and security for ourselves and our (hoped-for) children. Looking back over thirty-two years, do we still call it sacrifice?

When you 'seek first his kingdom and his righteousness,' God has promised that 'all these things will be given to you' (Matthew 6:33). It is as we look at 'all these things' that we begin to see that we gained a great deal more than we lost. What are 'all these things'? They will be different for each one of us – tailor-made for our particular needs and more than commensurate with our sacrifice.

For us it is first and foremost the privilege of having been called to be in partnership (albeit very junior partners) with our all-powerful, miracle-working, heavenly Father. It is at the same time thrilling and humbling to realize that we were involved with God as he broke into one of Satan's strongholds. But it is more than that. We are amazed to think that, in order to give us a share in this task, God was prepared to perform a miracle to save Bill's life (in spite of our shaky faith). Then, years later, he took us back to Sabah. There he gave us the joy of hearing about it at a time when we were surrounded by many hundreds of Tagals whom *he* had liberated from the grip of Satan, yet who were constantly calling us 'Mum and Dad'. It came home to us that, on the one hand, we were the ones who first told them about the gospel but, on the other hand, God had done it all.

God and company

It is an extraordinary privilege to be taken into such a partnership when we are so inadequate for it. God does not expect us to be perfectly in tune with him. He meets us where we are, not where we think we should be or where others think we should be. Not even where he would like us to be. He then adapts himself to our particular limitations (lack of faith in our case). But he does not leave us where we are. He leads us on step by step, not seeming to mind how long it takes. There will be pruning (the cutting back of God-given growth to allow for new development) and that may mean sacrifice and pain. There will be learning through our mistakes and failures as well as through successes. The way will be different for each one but we will all be able to look back and see how much we have learnt along the way and particularly that we have learnt to know God better.

As if that is not enough, there is much more besides. Our lives have been enriched by new friends and new cross-cultural experiences. In the good as well as the bad times, we've seen God making 'all things work together for good' (Romans 8:28, AV). We are even privileged to have two of our daughters say that it was good to be brought up as missionaries' children because they too learnt so much. Even in material things we have proved that God is no man's debtor.

We look back and say that it seemed (and indeed was) real sacrifice at the time, in many different ways. But in retrospect, we have to say it was not, because we have learnt so much and benefited so much. And God took us into partnership with himself. There are still some things that we do not understand, but God has 'paid us the intolerable compliment of loving us',[1] and one day we will

---

[1] C. S. Lewis, *The Problem of Pain* (Fontana, 1957), p.29.

understand. In the meantime, we are just hugely thankful that he called us to work with him in East Malaysia.

To think about

1. 'I worked harder than all of them,' says Paul, 'yet not I, but the grace of God that was with me' (1 Corinthians 15:10).

   Consider partnership with God in (a) Joshua 1:1–5 (*I* will give...*you* set your foot...); (b) Matthew 28:18–20 (All authority... Therefore go...).

2. Do we value God's gifts of concentration, learning capacity, good health and the like, which have enabled us to succeed, more than our relationship to God who gave the gifts? Look at Philippians 3:7–10, and John 21:15 (if 'these' is taken to refer to the fish, i.e. the results of God's blessing on our professional career).

Bookshelf

Power Evangelism: Signs and Wonders Today, John Wimber (Hodder and Stoughton, 1985).
This book makes a valuable contribution to increasing our expectations of what God is willing to do to demonstrate his power in order to bring men and women to himself. It is well worth reading, but should be balanced with books such as those recommended at the end of chapter 12, which deal with suffering for the Lord's sake.

Signs and Wonders Today, Donald Bridge (IVP, 1985).
A sympathetic look at the subject, based on much personal experience, seeking to look at the scriptural principles. As the cover states: 'Cobwebs of disbelief and clouds of sensationalism will be swept away in equal quantities by this book.'

The Problem of Pain, C. S. Lewis (Fontana, 1957).
A classic which needs to be read and re-read, especially the chapter on 'Divine Goodness', where Lewis discusses our wrong conceptions of God's love.

2

Living 'by faith'

Yes, but… ●*A special party* ●*A surprise* ●*Provisions indeed* ●*Python and wild pig* ●*God's care* ●*Pitfalls*

'That's absolutely ridiculous,' I exploded, when Bill came back from seeing the President of the Council of the Borneo Evangelical Mission (BEM). Harold McCracken had just asked us to do a nine-week deputation tour of Victoria, New South Wales and Queensland before leaving Australia for Borneo.

'You could earn enough in nine weeks to pay for both our fares and all the equipment that we need to go to Borneo *and* several months' allowance,' I continued. 'It seems silly to expect people to give gifts to us when we are quite capable of paying our own way.'

I was steamed up! Deep-down, I was dreading losing that last little bit of security before becoming dependent on the giving of God's people as we set out on our missionary career, but I was finding it quite easy to rationalize the situation. Bill, in his usual calm and reassuring way, agreed with me that on the surface it did seem a bit odd.

'But,' he added, 'we have been asked to do it and we can't really refuse. God is doing exciting things in Borneo and it really would be good to have the opportunity of talking about it and stimulating more interest.'

'Maybe,' I said, not wanting to be convinced. We had been married for just nine months and I didn't mind at all that a lot of folk had kindly given us money instead of presents for our wedding because we were going overseas. I was happy that we had used it all to pay for our fare to Australia to do the Wycliffe Linguistics course in Melbourne. The course was not yet available in England and so we either had to go to the States or to Australia. If we were going to work with an Australian mission, it seemed sensible to go to Melbourne and see something of the home end of the Mission.

In the first three weeks in Australia, Bill had earned enough money to add to our savings to pay for the course, but it had left us without enough to get to Borneo. Nevertheless we felt every penny of it had been well spent. It had given us the privilege of working for three months under the leadership and tuition of Dr Kenneth Pike, pioneer of some of the techniques for reducing as-yet-unwritten languages to writing. We had often said during the course that we felt like pinching ourselves to make sure we were not dreaming. It was so unbelievably good. The techniques were so simple yet profound and effective. The teaching methods were excellent. Ken Pike was an exciting lecturer and a thought-provoking conversationalist.

Yes, but...

We were both raring to get on with the job. But the BEM was a 'faith mission'. One of the seals of God's

19

call to anyone joining the Mission was their ability to meet the fares to get to Borneo, the first month's support once there, and the equipment needed for living in a tropical country. With a further well-paid locum in a general practice for another nine weeks, we had no problems at all to meet these requirements. But where would the money come from if we spent the whole nine weeks travelling around Australia taking a few meetings?

Eventually I came to see that Bill was right and we needed to do the deputation. We were members of the Mission now and to turn down a request (albeit only a request) such as we'd just received, would hardly have been a good start to our missionary careers. We had already shown a somewhat independent streak by convincing the Mission that we should get married before going to Borneo. The norm at that time was for engaged couples to wait to get married until after the initial period of adjustment and language-learning (a policy which, I am glad to say, was soon changed). I agreed reluctantly, whilst still rationalizing the situation.

'Even if God does give us the money, just think of all those gifts which could go to the rest of the work which needs money so badly. God will have to divert money to us which you could so easily have earned.'

I had not yet really registered that God had said 'the cattle on a thousand hills' are his (Psalm 50:10) and he was not hard pressed to find a few extra pounds!

A special party

I was still chuntering inside a few days later when we

went to a farewell party given by Ralph Davis (a BEM council member) and his wife Dulce. Ralph's mother and father had been our Australian 'Mum and Dad' ever since we'd arrived in Melbourne some four months earlier and we had grown to love all the family. Ralph and Dulce had recently taken over the big old family home which was becoming too much for the older couple, and so it was they who gave us the farewell.

It was a lovely evening. Harold McCracken and the BEM family in Melbourne had so generously taken these two 'pommies' (the popular term in Australia indicating a plum-in-mouth Englishman) to their hearts. Any argument I had with the Mission was forgotten that evening as we shared in the warmth of their love and kindness. It turned out to be something of a watershed in our experience of being missionary candidates.

There was one lady there whom we had met several times. We had been silently critical of her appearance until one day, maybe sensing our feelings, Ralph had explained:

'Mary [not her real name of course] is a great lady. She never spends anything on herself that she doesn't really have to, so that she can give to the Lord. She gives far more than she can afford.'

So that was why she always looked as if her clothes came from a not-very-good jumble sale. We had felt small and ashamed when we'd heard that and had said sorry to the Lord.

The party began to break up and Ralph suggested that we should stand in the hall to say goodbye. One by one we parted with our new friends, wondering whether we would ever see them again. Nearly last of all (because she had been helping Dulce to clear up) came Mary. She assured us of her prayers and we knew she meant it. But as she did so, she gripped my hand and pressed a note into it. After our confused and truly grateful thanks, she too disappeared into the night.

The hall where we were standing was dimly lit and I just slipped the note into my wallet. In all the busyness of that evening and the next morning, it didn't occur to me to look at it, though I thought about it a lot. I just assumed that it was a £1 note. But we did tell the Lord again that we were very sorry that we had been so critical of one of his very special saints.

Next day we set off for our first assignment. We were to be house-parents at the Warracknabeal convention (the Keswick of Northern Victoria). Ralph had generously lent us one of his firm's spacious Holden estate cars. It was big and comfortable and so suitable for the long journeys which we were going to have to do for the next nine weeks – quite a contrast to the little Austin Seven we had left behind in England. It was lovely to have a car of our own once more and to know we had some long journeys with no-one to interrupt our privacy. It was late summer and we opened all the windows to enjoy the warm Australian breezes blowing through our hair. We had responsibility ahead of us, but for the rest of the day we were free to talk, to enjoy each other's company and to enter into the new experience of the Australian bush.

A surprise

We enjoyed the sight of miles of gum-trees with their strangely unfamiliar ethereal appearance and the scent which every Australian tries to imagine when away from home. We were amazed by the miles and miles of long straight roads with no villages to slow us down. We had the excitement of seeing our first kangaroo in the bush rather than in a zoo. We unsuccessfully strained our eyes for a koala, and we talked. Of course we thought about the lovely farewell the night before and we mentioned Mary – not this time to criticize her! I idly picked up my wallet to look at the £1 note. It was a lot of money for someone in her position in 1952 and she really did not know us very well. But she knew we were off to Borneo and that was enough for her.

I opened my wallet and there, just where I had put it the night before, lay the note. It was a slightly different colour from our green English £1 notes, but about the same shape and size. It was greeny blue.

'Oh, no!' I exclaimed, nearly making Bill swerve. 'It's a five!' I added unbelievingly, as I thought of the large, crinkly white five-pound notes used in England at that time, notes which we'd seen but never actually used ourselves.

'Yes, it really is a five,' I went on as I examined it more closely. Bill stopped the car to have a look.

'Five pounds. She can't afford it. And she's given it to us!' There in the middle of the Australian bush, we bowed our heads and said a deep, deep thank-you – and prayed for Mary.

Before the weekend was over, with no-one knowing that we needed money (the Mission did not believe it was right to tell anyone our needs), God provided for us twice as much as Bill could have earned in over a week, however well-paid the locum might have been. We gave him back a tenth of each gift, but it seemed the more we gave, the more God

23

gave to us. So the story continued during the next nine weeks until we seemed to have all that we needed.

Provisions indeed

Our last assignment – foretaste of things to come – was to be house-parents and speakers at a weekend houseparty with some students. They gave us our board and lodging free in a beautiful 'out-back' type conference centre and we had a good time together. We were only a few years older than they were but they listened intently and we had some good discussions. They became quite excited about missions and they decided to give us a thank-you present in addition to our board. Their collection came to ten shillings and sixpence, and when we got back to Melbourne we found that with it we could just buy a large water urn. We had forgotten that that was felt to be an essential item for storing water which, being drawn from fairly dirty rivers, had to be boiled before we could drink it.

We were beginning to learn a lesson which would be repeated again and again over the next fifteen years in particular, but really for the rest of our lives. God delights to be no man's debtor. What had looked like sacrifice turned out to be the first exciting steps in 'living by faith' with regard to material things, but it was not always going to be that easy.

The Mission policy was to divide whatever came in between the various pressing needs for finance. Petrol for the aeroplane was a very high priority. Much of our work ground to a halt if we lost our mobility. The children's hostel had to be kept running. There were the day-to-day running expenses of the Mission. Missionaries' personal allowances were low on the list. It was not exceptional, in our early years, to go two months without an allowance at all. At other times it was a quarter or sometimes a half. To have two or three months in a row with a full allowance was unusual. We sometimes received personal gifts and often it was those who had just had a gift who helped those without. Or sometimes it was the local people whom God used to give us food because they understood what it was like to be without.

Python and wild pig

On one occasion when we had had no allowance, things were very tight. Bill was called to an urgent medical case three miles upriver. It was fairly late in the day. Normally sick people would come to him, but this time he felt he should go. I was not so sure.

'You can't go off and leave me with three small children and nothing to eat!' I protested. 'There's only enough in the cupboard for breakfast. Why should you go off and help someone else when your wife and family are in need?' Had I learnt anything over the years?

'I'll only be away one night. Eat what there is. I'll be back in the morning and I'm sure the Lord will provide for lunch when the time comes.' Bill prayed with me and off he went.

He'd not been in the village long and was in the middle of examining the patient when there was quite a commotion – people rushing in, grabbing their guns, calling dogs, rushing off into the jungle.

'What's happening?' Bill enquired.

'Someone has just come home and told us he's seen some wild pig tracks. We haven't seen wild pig for months. They've gone off to find them,' was the reply.

This was a great event. After the excitement had died down, all who were left settled down to the evening meeting and Bill was asked to preach. They listened well and talked long into the night. After a final look at the patient, Bill got out his sleeping-mat and mosquito-net and was soon asleep. He didn't hear the hunting party come back in the early hours of the morning.

After a good breakfast of rice and wild pig, Bill examined his patient. He was a good deal better and Bill decided it was time to leave for home. The villagers all lined up (as they so often do) eager to shake his hand and say goodbye. He'd seen quite a few others with minor ailments and they were all very grateful for his visit.

'*Tabek*.[Greetings.]' Someone shook his hand and gave him a bunch of bananas.

'*Tabek*. Thank you for coming,' and the speaker gave him a bunch of vegetables.

Others just shook his hand. A relative of the sick man gave him a four-gallon tin of rice; another gave him a whole leg of pork. They had brought back only one pig which would be divided between the whole village, but one of the back legs had been set aside for Bill – such is their generosity. Yet another gave him a 12 lb hunk of python steak! They had followed the pig tracks into the jungle and instead of finding a pig they had found a python. It was curled up and very, very sleepy. When they had killed it, they found the pig inside. The tracks were so fresh that they knew the pig had only just been swallowed, so it was perfectly edible!

Bill had come home laden with food, enough for many days. It had been given to him by those who were so much worse off than we were. They wanted to show their gratitude, and God wanted to show us he could look after us whether we had an allowance or not.

God's care

On another occasion it was our turn to be the benefactors, without fully knowing how great the need was. We were comfortably off that month, having had a personal gift from friends at home. We had noticed one or two things which made us think the pilot and his wife were having a struggle. We invited them and their children to supper and made it a substantial meal. We had a lovely time of fellowship and they went off home.

'My, those kids ate well, didn't they?' I commented to Bill after they had gone.

'Yes, I've never known them eat so well. They're growing up fast,' Bill replied.

It was not just that they were growing up. Several days later, when the crisis was over, we were talking to Bruce and Ruth.

'You know, your meal was the only real meal we had that day,' Ruth admitted. 'How did you know we were short?'

'I don't really know, but I think the Lord prodded us,' I replied. And Bruce went on to tell how they had sat down at lunchtime to give thanks for a glass of water. Half an hour later he had been given a bunch of bananas and he had jumped on his bike to chase up the kids who had gone off to play. He gave them each a couple of bananas.

'You should have seen the surprise and delight on their faces when I gave them the bananas. And then you invited us for supper. What answers to prayer. They, and we, learnt something of our Father's care that day.'

It wasn't always like that of course. Sometimes we would have several months without a crisis, but we all learnt to live economically.

It was one thing to live like that when all of our friends were doing the same and it was so exciting to see time and again the Lord meeting our needs in unexpected ways. How were we going to cope when God called us back to England? We had already noticed that we were being left behind in the material rat race. We were chatting one day with friends from another mission.

'Have you noticed,' one of them commented, 'how on your first leave, you found your friends had bought a house and a car, then on your second leave, they'd moved to a bigger house and the wife had a car?'

'Yes, we have noticed.'

'And on your third leave, the carpets will be thicker,' they added somewhat cynically.

Fifteen years after leaving England, having seen God establish over twenty churches amongst the Tagals, having helped to bring about a health revolution and having translated a New Testament for them, we came home to take up life in England again. With three children and moving towards the age when many at home were in mid-career, we had no home, no job, no car, and very little money. We had certainly learnt to live simply, but would that suffice in Western society?

Waiting for us at the airport was a brand new car – the folk who gave it to us had been going to have a new one but had kept their old one. A member of what was to become our church lent us a rent-free house for a year. A year later we were given a large cheque by a couple not from our church and told to go and buy a four-bedroomed house with central heating. Our handicapped daughter had been given a trust for as long as she needed the income. The other two were given their education in a small independent school because their upbringing in Borneo had left them unprepared initially for the rough-and-tumble of secondary schooling in England. And Bill, who had been virtually out of medicine for fifteen years, was able to find a job with the child-health services, working with families with handicapped children. Within three years he was back on a level with his peer group.

We had seemed to sacrifice so much materially when we left home. We experienced tough situations, shortages, uncertainties as to how God would provide. But he always did, even if it was sometimes at the very last minute. In this way we learnt, slowly and sometimes reluctantly, to live by faith. Each time God allowed us to be in situations where our faith was stretched, we learnt to trust him a little more with the result that our faith became just a little bit stronger.

Pitfalls

We also learnt that there were pitfalls in the very process of learning these lessons. A visitor had arrived at our headquarters one day. She told us that she had mentioned to someone in the capital, Kuching, that she was about to visit us.

'Oh, look out!' she had been warned. 'Tighten your belt. They are tough up there and they enjoy it.'

Was that true, we wondered. Were we in danger of being proud of our ability (albeit with God's help) to survive on very little? Perhaps we should not keep the aircraft flying at all costs? Certainly when some younger missionaries joined us in the late 60s and early 70s they were alarmed by the tough attitude to 'living by faith'. We are thankful to say that, with the merger with the Overseas Missionary Fellowship (OMF), there has come a much more balanced attitude to missionaries' allowances while still keeping the stress on 'looking to God alone'.

There was another more serious side-effect of our attitudes. Because we never asked for money – other than in prayer to God – we found it very difficult to talk about money. We rarely felt free to teach the responsibility for giving (either in the churches in Borneo or at home). The result of this was that many a pastor left the ministry due to lack of support, or even if they stayed in, they quite often spent so much time rearing pigs or planting rubber that they didn't have nearly enough time for their pastoral duties. The churches were happier with a 'part-time' pastor than having to raise money to support him and his family.

Now that we are on the giving end rather than on the receiving end, we feel the attitude of those of us at home must be that the 'worker deserves his wages' (Luke 10:7). Certainly we proved that God is no man's debtor. But as we work in partnership with him, it is our responsibility to see that we do not neglect our part in seeing that those in full-time service (both at home and overseas) are adequately cared for – and that does not mean living on the bread-line.

To think about

1. Interdenominational Faith Missions were started by Hudson Taylor of the China Inland Mission in order not to divert money from the denominational missions. 'We look to God alone to supply our needs.' How can we trust God to do that without making any appeals? (Philippians 4:12, 19)

2. Is this the only way for a missionary society to run its finances? What other scriptural ways are there of supporting God's work? (1 Corinthians 16:1-3; Philippians 4:14-18; 2 Corinthians 8:1-5)

3. Either way missionaries are dependent on the giving of God's people. How much should we give to God's work? (Malachi 3:8-10; 1 Corinthians 16:2; 2 Corinthians 9:7; 1 Timothy 5:8)

Note on Malachi 3: The tithes required by the Mosaic law were, first a tenth of all that remained after the first-fruits (which belonged to God and must be given to him). This tenth was also God's and was paid to the Levites for their maintenance (Leviticus 27:30-32). From this tenth the Levites paid a tenth to the priests (Numbers 18:26-28). Secondly, a second tenth was paid by the people for the entertainment of the Levites and their own families at the tabernacle (Deuteronomy 12:17-19). Thirdly, another tenth was paid every third year for the poor, the widows and orphans (Deuteronomy 14:28-29). Over and above this were the free-will offerings.

Bookshelf

Take my life, Michael Griffiths (IVP, 1967; now jointly published with STL).
A book for those who want to '[press] on day by day, more and more eagerly enjoying life with Christ'. It deals with many aspects of the Christian life. Chapter 4 is an especially helpful study on our attitude to money.

Pennies for Heaven, Ian Coffey (Kingsway Publications, 1984).
An important book for our twentieth-century church which is infiltrated by the materialistic society in which we live. Can we sing 'Our God reigns' and not allow him to direct our attitude to material possessions? Ian Coffey grasps the nettle of giving, and calls us to acknowledge the Lordship of Christ over all of our life. Our giving, he suggests, then 'flows from that fundamental relationship'.

To a Different Drum, Pauline Hamilton (OMF Books, 1984).
An exciting autobiography of a missionary with a PhD in physiology. When God prevented Pauline Hamilton from taking her own life, she began to 'dance to a different drum' and followed God's call to China. Particularly relevant to our subject in this chapter are the two chapters 'Does God still pro-

vide?' and 'Loaves and fishes', in which she tells of God's miraculous provision for two consecutive young people's conferences. This was after the money collected to run them had all been stolen from her house.

Biography of James Hudson Taylor, Dr and Mrs Howard Taylor (Hodder and Stoughton and OMF Books, 1973).
This is an abridged version of the story of how God led Hudson Taylor to 'look to God alone' for the provision of all his needs as he founded the China Inland Mission (now the OMF) in order to reach the peoples of inland China.

3

Guidance

Meeting Bill • Married or single? • My own battles •
Wycliffe – and choices

What were two 'pommies' doing joining a small
Australian mission which had no connections with
the United Kingdom? Why not go somewhere in
south-east Asia where the Overseas Missionary Fellowship was working? After all Bill's first missionary
giving had gone to OMF. He'd managed to save 120
old pennies by walking one mile of his journey to
university each day and saving a penny a day on the
journey. After that he'd really prayed for those missionaries to whom he had given such hard-earned
money. 'For where your treasure is, there your heart
will also' (Matthew 6:21). My first interest in missions was aroused through the two-volume biography of Hudson Taylor, and several other OMF
books on south-west China. So why not join a mission for which we had prayed, and to which we had
given our money, and where many of our fellow-
workers would be from Great Britain?

Quite simply (if guidance is ever simple) we
believed that God had called us to Borneo. As we
had thought about the BEM we discovered that it
had been founded on the same principles and prac-

tices as the OMF. Three young men would have loved to go to Borneo under the auspices of the China Inland Mission (as it was called in those days). But as its name suggests, in 1928 the CIM did not believe that God had called them to work beyond the confines of inland China. So the young men had started the new Mission. We were happy to apply to such a Mission, and its leadership agreed that God had called us. They had been praying for some time for a doctor and a translator to join the team and we seemed to fit the need. But how had we got to that point?

It was a long and slow process, and marriage was a particular complication. Bill and I had actually qualified the same year from different universities, Bill's medical qualification having taken two years longer than my German degree. Bill had succeeded in getting himself seconded to the Colonial Medical Service instead of doing national service (still compulsory in the immediate post-war years).

'Why go into the army as a medical officer in peace time to look after some of his Majesty's fittest citizens?' he'd argued with himself. 'There are thousands of his Majesty's most needy citizens in some of the "colonial" areas. They are in urgent need of medical attention. I can be more use there.' The authorities had agreed and he had been drafted to Malaya (now West Malaysia).

Meeting each other

We met some six months before he was due to leave England. Bill was chief usher and I was chief bridesmaid at the wedding of one of his school friends to one of my university friends.

At a meal after the wedding, we talked of the possibility of my joining him and his brother Jim on a climbing holiday. The sister on one of the wards where Bill was working had recently been converted and it seemed a good opportunity to invite her too. I had never done any rock climbing in my life but as I was fond of all sport it sounded an attractive invitation.

'Stop letting the rope out,' I yelled in vain on the third day. Jim, secured some fifty feet above me, and out of sight, had felt a tug on the rope and thought I was asking for it to be let out. In fact I'd slipped but Jim could not see me. Gently, marvellously gently, he let out the rope and slowly I went down and down until I came to rest on a ledge twenty-five feet below. With the rope slackened, Jim peered over the edge.

I looked somewhat helplessly at that extra twenty-five feet I now had to climb. I was enjoying my introduction to rock climbing, but it does have a way of using every muscle in the body and I was tired at the thought of having to do more than anyone else that day. When we woke to pouring rain the next morning, I was glad of an excuse to stay at home. Bill and Jim went out alone.

That night they came home soaked, dishevelled, tired and thoroughly happy. They'd had a rough and invigorating day without two women to hold them up. It was the first time I'd seen Bill anything but tidy. (Our meetings before the holiday had been with him either in tails or in a white coat with a stethoscope sticking out of his pocket.) He somehow seemed much more human and I began to think he was rather special. The feeling became mutual over the next few months on the few visits he was able to make to London, so that when he left for Malaya we both knew that marriage was a real possibility. We had two years to think about it and letters went back and forth with ever-increasing frequency!

During Bill's second year in Malaya he naturally began to wonder what the next step should be. He assumed that as a Christian he should make an open offer to the Lord for home or overseas, in medicine or whatever the Lord had in mind. There were several possibilities, including a very pressing invitation to join a new Mission starting up in the Middle East.

'I will not take no for an answer, Bill,' an old school friend had written to him. 'God needs you there and we need you. Don't bury yourself in the National Health Service!'

'If that's what you want, Lord, I am available.' But there was no peace.

Then came another pressing and even more attractive invitation to open up a work with the International Fellowship of Evangelical Students (IFES) in the universities of Indonesia. It was very much the sort of work he would have liked to do. The need was apparent. The time seemed right.

'If that's what you want, Lord, I'm available.' But still no peace. The need alone did not constitute a call.

Married or single?

Then one day he was visiting a tough, hairy-chested New Zealand friend in Singapore. Gordon had been a bee-keeper and amateur boxer as well as a teacher in Bible College before coming to Singapore. His main work in Singapore was amongst service men and God was obviously using him to get alongside tough servicemen and giving him a real ability to lead many to Christ.

'The BEM needs people like you in Borneo, Bill,' he bluntly challenged.

'BEM? I've never heard of them.'

'A bunch of Aussies. They're working in the interior of Borneo.'

'Aussies? Then it's not for me. They wouldn't want a pommie doctor in their ranks.'

'Oh, they're not like that. They've even got Kiwis [New Zealanders]! They're a good bunch. You'd fit in.'

'Why do you think they need someone like me?'

'They are urgently looking for single men to take the gospel to the interior tribes. It's rough country and some of the girls find it difficult. God is doing amazing things there. You'd find it very exciting as well as worthwhile.'

Bill did not really hear the last remarks as he was thinking hard about the first statement.

'Lord, you know that I was thinking you were bringing Shirley into my life,' he prayed that night. 'But I've given you an open offer. If this is what you want, then I'm available. I'll go to Borneo single.'

As he prayed, he began to experience a real inner peace from the Lord that it was to be Borneo. But as he continued to pray, he also had a strange awareness that he was to be married first.

'No, Lord. I'll go single. I don't trust Bill Lees. I think it's more likely to be my own feelings that are saying "get married first". Gordon said they want single men. I'll go single, Lord.'

The feeling persisted and he continued to distrust it, but he decided to work towards Borneo and see what happened. He did consider a visit to Borneo from Malaya but decided that that would not be right. It would be better to go to Australia and see the home end of the Mission. He couldn't consider joining a group he knew nothing about.

A few months later, shortly before Bill left Malaya for Australia, the BEM changed its policy. The single men were having so much difficulty in one area where it was considered right and proper for the local girls to make sexual advances to the men, the Mission decided they couldn't use single men any more in that area. They decided to pray for married couples!

'Lord, I've got the message, thank you,' Bill prayed gratefully.

My own battles

He had said very little of this in his letters during that six months. I knew of his missionary concern and he had mentioned Borneo several times but I did not know how sure he was and I was having battles of my own.

I'd thought very seriously about mission when I'd first read Hudson Taylor's biography shortly after my recommitment to the Lord in my second term at university. Missionary meetings however did not inspire me and I'd soon let the idea drift into the back of my mind. I taught for an experimental year after graduating, expecting to do a Certificate of Education the following year if I found that teaching suited me. (I had always said I would never teach!) I had enjoyed it and had almost decided to take up the place offered to me for the Certificate of

Education. Then, somewhat out of the blue, I had a letter from the Scripture Gift Mission. I went for an interview and it seemed right to all of us that I should give up my brief teaching career.

Mission interest obviously revived through being at the SGM. I read Isobel Kuhn's *Nests Above the Abyss* and the story of J. O. Fraser in *Beyond the Ranges* (now rewritten as *Mountain Rain*). I began to 'dream' about going to the tribes of south-west China and using my love of languages to translate a Bible for them. China's borders then closed and my dream came to an abrupt end.

Reality began to dawn when I was asked to write a series of twelve articles for the SGM children's magazine on translation projects in various parts of the world. I thoroughly enjoyed the research and the writing – except for one which I kept putting off. I wrote the one on Borneo last. I didn't seem to want to find out too much about it. Eventually I had to get down to it and I discovered that the BEM was very similar to the OMF. Perhaps even more significantly they were involved in translation work and wanting to do more. It was a tribal situation not dissimilar to south-west China. It seemed obvious that it was the sort of place and the sort of mission where I could work and where I could translate a New Testament. In fact it seemed a bit too obvious and I didn't really like it. It was all very well to dream but I decided that I didn't want to go overseas in reality. In fact I very much wished Bill would stop talking about Borneo in his letters.

After considerable battling, I eventually told the Lord I was willing to go to Borneo if that was what he wanted. I then had the problem of deciding whether this was really God calling me or whether it was just because I wanted to marry Bill. Was I willing to go single? I didn't know. Eventually I decided I needed to prove to myself that I was willing to go single, whether Bill was called to Borneo or not. I decided to write off to see if there was a place on the Wycliffe course in Australia. I posted the letter with some reluctance but felt a great sense of relief afterwards.

Wycliffe – and choices

About this time, Bill was on his way home making his long detour via Australia. He had never heard of Wycliffe when he arrived in Melbourne but Harold McCracken, the Chairman of the BEM, was talking a lot about it. He had been one of the men instrumental in getting Wycliffe to Melbourne and they were all very excited about it.

'Bill, you need Wycliffe in England. We hear there has been some sort of blockage in the correspondence and negotiations. What about you having a go at unblocking it?'

He gave Bill two letters explaining the benefits of the course and suggested he gave one to the Principal of London Bible College and one to the SGM. The more Bill heard about Wycliffe, the more he thought it would be a very useful thing for him to do if he was going to have to learn one or possibly two languages in Borneo.

Wycliffe – Borneo – the jigsaw puzzle pieces were looking strangely similar. We became engaged within a few weeks of Bill's arrival in England, and over the next weeks the Lord graciously confirmed the decision many times over.

We had both come to the point of being willing to stay single but in the end we were grateful to discover that God was giving us an 'Abramic' experience. When God asked Abraham to offer up Isaac, he was testing his willingness and trust. He knew he was going to provide the ram. In the same way he was asking for our willingness, not actually asking us to make that particular sacrifice. He has however asked many of our friends to give up the prospect of marriage in order to serve him overseas. The single person in an isolated cross-cultural situation faces a special sort of loneliness, but God has used very many of them in special ways. As Paul suggests in 1 Corinthians 7, the single person cares in a unique way for the things of the Lord whereas the married couple has a particular temptation to get preoccupied with family. It is not for us to say how God enables each individual to look back and say, 'It's not sacrifice' and some may well not be able to until they receive their abundant reward in heaven. But reward there certainly will be.

We had jumped the 'singleness' hurdle – but life was still not going to be plain sailing. While at home Bill decided to visit his former medical school. He had developed something of a friendship with Professor Frazer whom he regarded very highly.

'Bill, we can find you something better than that,' was the Professor's comment when Bill explained he was thinking of going to Borneo. 'Why don't you come and join me on my team? I have a space for someone like you.'

What an attractive offer! Had it come a few months earlier, Bill would have been very keen to accept. But God had really been confirming to us that Borneo was the place where he wanted us, and

Bill was sure it was right to turn down the one job in the whole of England that he would have most liked.

Several of our friends have had similar offers when they have set their faces towards mission. The man who became Chairman of the BEM was offered dramatic promotion if only he'd stay in the company. A young friend who joined the OMF a few years ago was offered what he saw as the number one job in his field in any university in England. He was invited to a lectureship and to do further research in the field in which he had done his PhD and had already published extensively. The enemy argument is 'You can serve God better in a prestigious appointment!' Of course that is true if that is what the Lord wants. But the key to usefulness is obedience, not status.

Family opposition was the next hurdle we had to face. My parents viewed the idea of our going to Borneo with apprehension. They were delighted with their prospective son-in-law but were none too keen on his taking their daughter off to Borneo.

'You must do what you think is right. It's your life. We will not stand in your way' was the nearest they could get to approval of our going to Borneo.

But no such reluctant approval came from Bill's parents.

'It will kill me if you go to Borneo' was his mother's rebuff.

What were we to do? We knew that the Bible said we were to honour our parents. We were 'of age' so we did not need to obey them. But honouring parents is something which lasts a lifetime.

We agreed to stay in the United Kingdom for one year 'to think further'. We waited and prayed. In fact our refusal to apply to BEM was somewhat misunderstood in Australia.

'You're losing your vision now you are home, Bill' was one comment which came in a letter from Melbourne.

We waited the full year. We were married, and Bill took a registrarship in South London while I continued to work at the SGM. Only then did we apply to BEM. After further discussion with Bill's parents it became obvious that they greatly appreciated our willingness to comply with their wish that we should not 'rush' into such a major step.

When we finally set off for Australia and the Wycliffe course some twelve months after Bill had returned to England (Wycliffe did get off the ground in England, but not until a year later), Bill's parents were not only reconciled to our going. They came to see us off, and we left with their blessing. We took this as yet another confirmation that it was God who was calling us to Borneo.

To think about

1. Why does the need not constitute a call? See Ephesians 2:10; Matthew 9:36-38; Revelation 3:7; Proverbs 3:5-6; Psalm 32:8-9.

2. Is it right to consider family pressures when considering missionary service overseas? Compare Luke 14:26-27 with Luke 2:49-52 and John 19:25-27. Also compare Matthew 12:46-50 with Matthew 15:3-9, 1 Timothy 5:8 and Ephesians 6:2.

3. God guided Bill and myself very differently. In

what ways does God adapt his guidance to individual personalities? Look at Joshua 1:1-9; Jeremiah 1:4-10; Jonah 1:1-2 and 3:1-2; Matthew 4:18-22; Acts 9:1-9; Acts 13:2-3. These are just a selection. Find some more passages.

Bookshelf

Give me this mountain, Helen Roseveare (IVP, 1966; now jointly published with STL).
A frank and often humorous account of the battles and triumphs of a young Christian who then obeyed God's call to be a missionary. In chapters 8 and 9 Helen Roseveare discusses her first leave and the struggles she had as she faced up to the problem of singleness.

'Dear Mum and Dad...': How to honour your parents, Chua Wee Hian (IVP, 1984).
A helpful study on our attitude to parents by the General Secretary of the International Fellowship of Evangelical Students. He calls on his vast experience of counselling students as he helps us to see what the Bible teaches.

When God guides, edited by Denis Lane (OMF Books, Living Testimony Series, 1984).
A collection of stories showing how God guides different people in a variety of ways. The book has a most useful introduction in which Denis Lane sets out ten principles for knowing God's guidance.

A Hitch-hiker's Guide to Mission, Ada Lum (IVP/STL joint edition, 1985; US edition IVP/USA, 1984).

Based on many of her own experiences, Ada Lum challenges and encourages us all to consider mission at home and overseas. 'Obedience on earth expands our capacities to enjoy heaven', she concludes.

4

Why is guidance so difficult?

Comfort in a storm ● *Indecision* ● *A fresh testing* ●
'Guidance gets harder' ● *A reliable guide*

'Without faith it is impossible to please God' (Hebrews 11:6). God wants to guide us but he also wants us to exercise faith. Sometimes his leading will be abundantly clear. There will also be other times when we have to take a step of faith, not knowing what the following step will be.

For a number of years we were very sure of God's leading in all our major decisions and in some of the smaller ones. Along with thousands of other missionaries (and many at home too) we experienced the thrill of step-by-step guidance. Even if we had struggles, as we looked back, we were certain God had led.

'I wouldn't have minded if there had been a thousand people in the church. I know we were in God's plan,' was the assurance with which I spoke about our wedding some months afterwards.

We were quite sure that God led us to Borneo. We had battles and testings, but we experienced the peace of God ruling our hearts (Philippians 4:7). Later, as we reached the Tagal people, we were sure that that was where we should be. On our first leave,

47

we didn't want to take it for granted that God wanted us back in Borneo. We never wanted to say, 'Lord, you have led us this way. We will not listen to any change of direction.'

We therefore prayed for a re-commissioning and we asked that it should be just as clear as our first call to Borneo.

Comfort in a storm

It was when we were visiting Northern Ireland for some meetings that God answered our prayer. The night before we were due to sail back it was cold, so I got into bed to have my evening 'quiet time'. I sat up in bed listening to the wind howling round the house where we were staying. I remembered the last time I had visited Ireland. Bill had been speaking at the Bangor Convention shortly after we were engaged, and my sister and I had gone to Ireland to join up with him for a holiday after the Convention. We had had a terrible crossing. Our boat was one of the very few to set out and the Captain and my sister were the only ones on board not to be seasick! It was the sort of night where at first you are afraid you are going to die and then you are feeling so awful that you wish you could die. The only thing that had kept me remotely cheerful was the thought of Bill waiting on the quayside. And here we were again having to face that crossing in a storm. I was scared.

I picked up my Bible and turned to my daily reading. I had reached the point in Mark's Gospel where he relates the story of the storm on the Sea of Galilee. What a comfort to be reminded that Jesus was still the same. He was in control. After prayer and thanking the Lord for his word, we turned out the light and were dozing off to sleep.

'You have just found my word comforting, haven't you?' God seemed to be saying to me.

'Yes, Lord. Thank you for it.'

'If you who are well acquainted with the Bible still found you were afraid until you actually read a familiar passage, then go back to the Tagals. Translate the New Testament for them, so that they can read it in their own language. Then they too can learn from it and be comforted by it.'

The message was as clear as if I had actually heard God's voice. I roused myself enough to share what had happened with Bill. We discussed it, prayed about it and then both went off into a peaceful sleep.

We woke next morning with the continued assurance that it had been the Lord speaking to me and giving us the confirmation for which we had been asking. As a little bonus, the wind had died down and we had a lovely crossing!

We enjoyed this certainty of knowing God's will but we were not exceptions in the group of young people amongst whom we were working in the BEM. They were an excellent team. God had been doing great things. We were all in partnership with him and with one another. We prayed and expected God to direct us. The daily 7 a.m. prayer meeting at headquarters was central to our thinking and to the work. We never wanted to step away from the centre of God's will. It was great!

Indecision

Time and again we 'waited on the Lord' to see what

he wanted us to do. But gradually and almost imperceptibly we were slipping into a dangerous position. We didn't want to make a decison until we knew it to be God's will. We were drifting into what we have come to see as an 'occupational hazard' of missionaries who have experienced a great deal of clear-cut guidance. We were not prepared to make decisions after praying that he would direct our choosing. We were waiting for God to make our decisions for us.

We first really became aware of this when we were on leave wondering whether we should return to Borneo and leave our eldest daughter, Ruth, at home with friends in England. She was handicapped. We and the BEM leadership felt it was inappropriate to try to bring her up in Borneo with no possibility of special schooling which she needed. Again and again we prayed, we talked, we questioned, we read God's Word and we waited. In fact we stayed in England for two years. We had eight different offers to have Ruth, but none seemed right for all sorts of different reasons. Then we had an offer which looked as if it was what God wanted, and still we waited.

One day an ex-colleague from Borneo visited us and was perturbed at what he saw as our indecision.

'I don't know why you are making so much fuss about whether you should go back or not,' he said bluntly.

'What do you mean?' I replied, feeling that he had no understanding of the emotional turmoil that we were in.

'You say the indications are that you ought to go back. You have friends offering to have Ruth. Then it's simple. Make the decision to return and if it's

50

wrong, God has promised to speak.'

He was of course referring to Isaiah 30:21. It is only as we make the decision, as we 'turn to the right or to the left' that God promises that we will 'hear a voice behind you, saying, "This is the way; walk in it." '

We did a bit more thinking. Basically we did not want to say we should go back and leave Ruth. We were hiding behind a facade of spirituality. Eventually, recommitting ourselves to the Lord and his purposes for our lives, and looking at all the facts, we made the decision. We trusted that God would keep his promise of Isaiah 30. We 'heard' no contrary voice. Instead, God opened all sorts of doors to make it possible and to show us that it was in fact best for Ruth as well as for the Tagals.

A fresh testing

Six years later however we still had not really learnt our lesson about walking by faith. We were faced with a not dissimilar problem. We were at home in England and had stayed on because Ruth's condition had deteriorated considerably. For two years we had had no problem with guidance because we just had to stay in England. The other two girls were obviously benefiting enormously by our being at home with them but we were clearly staying on because of Ruth. After two years she died. We then had to face a new situation. If we had been staying only for Ruth, then should we not now pack our bags and return to Borneo? Again the turmoil.

'Lord, do you want us to leave the two girls and return to the Tagals?'

'Lord, we know it will be hard to leave them. But you blessed Ruth and she didn't suffer. We don't really want to give greater priority to the family than to the work to which you have called us.'

'Lord, when will you make it clear? We don't want to go, if you want us here. We don't want to stay if you want us in Borneo. What are we to do?'

We were really in just the same dilemma as before. But this time the evidence was pushing us in the direction of making a decision to stay at home because the girls needed us. For good evangelical missionaries that seemed to be a very 'unspiritual' decision. Surely God's call and God's work came first?

Eventually, again trusting the Lord to keep his promise of Isaiah 30:21, we made the decision – this time to stay. We did not deny our original call to Borneo. It was just that God was now, we believed, calling us to stay at home. He must have other plans for his church amongst the Tagals. Again there was no 'voice behind' saying we had made the wrong decision. There was nothing other than an immediate deep sense of peace and assurance that it was the Lord's prerogative to call to Borneo and to call back from Borneo.

We were learning more of walking by faith. Over the years we have seen the rightness of that decision both in terms of what God had given us to do, and in relation to the girls. We had to believe that God could meet the needs of the Tagals in another way.

For us the decision had been to stay at home. But God's leading and our circumstances were different from those of many of our friends who have rightly understood that God wanted them to continue over-seas. They have done just that, despite the many pulls to stay at home and the frequent heartaches of separations. God has honoured their decision. Equally he has honoured ours and opened up a sphere of service amongst young people, particularly students, where we have been able to encourage their faith and help them to consider service for the Lord at home and particularly overseas.

We were faced with a simple 'yes' or 'no' decision – the struggle was whether we were willing to do God's will. Were we willing for the criticism and lack of 'front-line' position by staying at home? Were we willing for the heartaches of separation by going back? Once the decision was made, it did seem remarkably simple because we had peace. But God gave no signs along the way.

'Guidance gets harder'

'Guidance gets harder and harder as you get older,' Oswald Sanders (the then Director of the OMF) explained to us one day when we sought his advice. He had gone on to explain how God wants us to walk by faith. Often when we first go out as missionaries, we are young and God allows guidance to be especially clear, sometimes even spectacular. But as we grow older, we learn to walk daily with him. We get to know him better. We know more of his priorities rather than ours. We make decisions within the context of our walking with God.

'In this situation,' he added, 'whatever you decide you will find some people say you are wrong.'

That was rather what we expected but strangely (or is it so strangely?) we can only remember two couples who ever said to us: 'Isn't it time you went back to Borneo?'

If we are to walk by faith, we need to know the one to whom we are entrusting our lives. The important question is, how well do we know God?

In Borneo, when we want to go into some new area, the first thing we do is look for a reliable guide. We look for a guide who knows the country, who knows the best path, and who will be able to help us cross the many rivers which will bar our way. We need a guide who can communicate with us, even if he does not understand our language completely or if we don't understand his fully. Then above all this, there is the need to find out if he is willing to be our guide. Is he reliable enough not to abandon us half-way? Once we've found the guide, really all we need to do is walk or climb behind him (he doesn't carry us!) and accept his helping hand across narrow bridges or rushing torrents.

Obviously we are taking a slight risk when we choose a human guide, but not when we have God as our guide. We find the answer to every question we can pose is 'God is able and God is willing to be our guide.'

He certainly knows the territory into which he is taking us. He knows every twist, turn and temptation that will face us. He knows the end from the beginning, and nothing will take him by surprise. (2 Chronicles 16:9; Hebrews 4:13; Revelation 1:8; etc.)

We also have clear evidence from Scripture that he is not only willing to be our Guide but wants to be. He has promised he will guide us. He is concerned that we should do his will. He is also highly competent to guide us because he knows us through and through. He knows our weaknesses. He knows the best route for people like us. He knows how fast we can go, how much we can take each day, how many obstacles we are able to face with his help. (Deuteronomy 33:25; Psalm 32:8; Psalm 139:1–4; Proverbs 3:5–6, margin; Ephesians 2:10.)

A reliable guide

God is also totally reliable as our Guide. He will stay with us on the journey even if we decide to take a turning contrary to his leading and don't turn back when we hear the 'voice behind us' – or even when we don't try to hear it. He will turn aside with us just as he did for Israel when they disobeyed him in asking for a king. It may be a more difficult route, and he may refine us through it, but he has promised he will not abandon us on it. He chose a king for Israel and then even used the monarchy to be the royal line for the incarnation of his son. (Deuteronomy 31:6; 1 Samuel 8:6–8, 19–22; Job 23:10; Malachi 3:3–4; Matthew 28:20; Hebrews 13:5.)

God can certainly be trusted as our Guide. But he does not do everything for us. As in the case of the human guide, we have to do the walking and the climbing. It is a partnership with God. As he said to Joshua, '*I* will give you every place where *you* set your foot' (Joshua 1:3).

Why then is it so difficult to give an open offer to such a Lord? – 'Anywhere, anytime, in any capacity, Lord.'

It must be that, in spite of all we have just said, we don't fully trust him. That sounds terrible when we put it like that, but it's true. We know he knows the situation. We know he knows us, with our weaknesses and our strengths. We know his power, his love, his understanding are sufficient. We know of his concern, his enabling, the gifts he has given us to do the job – why hesitate?

'Look out, he may take you into situations you can't cope with,' the enemy whispers in our ear. 'It may mean you have to stay single all your life. You'll be lonely and misunderstood.' Then to some he says, 'Look out, God is a Shylock. He wants his "pound of flesh". He wants cheap labour to do his work. It'll ruin your health, your happiness, your home. It's too big a risk. It's too great a sacrifice. You're not up to it.'

As we listen, we are paying more attention to the lies of the enemy than to the 'still small voice' of the Spirit. The enemy tells us that we are taking a risk in trusting God. Yet God has shown us time and time again that he is trustworthy and that he cares. He will only lead us within the context of our (his and our) best interests.

'But', you may say, 'if only I knew! Why can't God make it clearer, or be more explicit?'

He can and certainly he sometimes does. He can light up a burning bush and speak from it. He can write on a wall and lay on an interpreter. He can give dreams and visions and can speak audibly to us. He can even make the waters of the Red Sea divide and lead his people through. He can respond to a fleece which we lay before him and he can, and does still, do many other marvellous things. But even with spectacular guidance we still need to exercise faith if we are to please God. Spectacular guidance can be false, as we see from the activities of the false prophets.

There is evidence to suggest that Paul, on at least

one occasion, was more suspicious of spectacular guidance than of 'ordinary' guidance. In Acts 16 we read of how he had travelled across Asia Minor, seeking step-by-step guidance from the Holy Spirit. Within the context of ongoing commitment to the Lord and the command of Acts 1:8 they decided to go into Asia and Bithynia. As they moved forward they heard the 'voice behind them' saying 'No'. Then they came to Troas, where Paul had a vision. That surely would make the guidance clear-cut. But what was the first thing Paul did after receiving the vision? A careful study of the pronouns and the grammar of Acts 16:10 make it very clear that he consulted his travelling companions first. 'We got ready to leave...concluding that...' (Luke now includes himself in the narrative.) But it was not just that Paul told them and they all got ready to go. Notice the order. 'We got ready...concluding...' They concluded first, then got ready to go. Obviously Paul told his companions, they prayed and talked about the vision. They then concluded that it was from God and moved forward.

If we know the Guide, if we trust him and make an open offer to him, then he will guide us in the way which is most suitable for us. We shall need to exercise faith, sometimes to accept spectacular guidance which we need to check with our church or reliable Christians, sometimes to accept taking one step at a time, not quite knowing where the next step will lead us. But, in it all, God will expect us to use the minds which he has given us to make decisions along the way. And he will always remember and act on his promise of Isaiah 30:21.

To think about

1. God has no favourites. Guidance is for all. Those who make an open offer may expect his leading into missions, ministry, commerce, industry, the professions and the like. He has made us people, not robots, (Genesis 1:26–27). He has given us minds (Isaiah 1:18).

   Meditate on your open offer to the Lord.

2. Look up and study the many Bible references in this chapter.

Bookshelf

The Fight, John White (IVP, 1977; first published in the USA).
This is a helpful book for many aspects of the Christian life. The chapter on 'Guidance' is outstanding.

5

God, rebels and Executive Committees

*A long goodbye • Why us? • Meanwhile, on with
the job • Jungle fish and chips • Another's needs •
An unexpected solution*

Bill was getting thinner and thinner. A large bottle
of pills was almost empty and still the dysentery continued. He looked as if he had lost well over a stone
in weight but there was no means of telling, as we
were in one of the most remote parts of the country.

We were alone. We had no radio contact with headquarters. We had been in Borneo for no more than
nine months. The Executive Committee had asked
us to go to work with Ray Cunningham for a while
amongst the Kenyah tribe. The Sarawak Kenyah
live far up in the headwaters of the great Baram and
Rejang rivers which cut across the middle of the
country. We had greatly enjoyed working for a
month or two with our 'senior' missionary who had
pioneered the work in the Upper Baram.

Ray had in fact been in Borneo only three years
longer than we had, and he was about our age. In
the BEM of the fifties (described as 'a bunch of kids'
by one visitor), that made him our senior missionary.
There were only two men on the field executive who
had done more than a term (four years) of missionary service and one of them was at home on leave at

59

the time.

Ray, who had served in Borneo as a sapper in the Australian army, was a great pioneer missionary, constantly travelling, full of enthusiasm and well-loved by the Kenyah people. Through him, we too had been readily accepted by them. We were therefore not too dismayed when he had to leave us alone while he went out to the field executive meetings at Lawas. We went upriver with him to the pocket-handkerchief airstrip which he himself had helped to build some months before.

A long goodbye

As we waved him goodbye, we were all confident that he would be back within the week. We could survive that long even though we didn't speak a great deal of Kenyah and were still trying to learn the trade language Malay – though we were 'murdering' the latter quite effectively to make ourselves understood!

Three weeks later there was still no sign of him. The rivers had been high for the second week and as the journey to the airstrip was half a day's battle up the rapids, we were not too surprised that he had not returned. We were not even worried at first, in spite of Bill's illness. But as the days of the third and fourth weeks went by the situation was beginning to look a bit bleak. I was beginning to imagine the worst. Would Bill ever get better? What would happen if he became critically ill and still Ray had not returned? And what were we going to do about food? We had already been stretching our meagre supplies out for three weeks, and could not go on

much longer. Besides all this, we were feeling rebelli-
ous. The feeling kept nagging that our Mission
Executive had missed God's will in asking us to go to
the Kenyah 'to initiate a translation programme'.

We were working on our fourth tribal language in
nine months. What a privileged first year we were
having. Not only had we analysed the sounds of one
language in order to write it down, and checked
another which had been worked out by a linguistic-
ally-trained missionary, but we had also analysed the
alphabet and grammar of a third. We had enjoyed
the linguistics as well as the privilege of moving
around to the different language areas. It had given
us a wonderful introduction to the amazing work
that God was doing in Borneo. This time we were
learning and analysing Kenyah, so that we could
write it down and pave the way for the translation of
the Scriptures. We had certainly enjoyed Ray's company and would not have missed the experience of
working with him for anything. But that did not
alter our frustration and the feeling that we ought to
be moving on.

Why us?

We knew Ray needed some Scriptures for the new
Kenyah Christians. That was clear. He spoke the language well, and he had already begun to see the
church established. But he was a pioneer and he
could not see himself sitting down to a translation
job. I was convinced that God had called me to Borneo to translate a New Testament – so what was the
problem? We were in full agreement with the Executive that Ray needed help and we could give that to

him with the language analysis. But we had been feeling for a long time that God was calling us to the Tagals in Sabah. The Executive recognized this long term, but had asked us to 'initiate the translation' for the Kenyah first. To us that seemed like at least three years, and the Tagals had been waiting since before the war for someone to go and teach them. We indulged from time to time in the luxury of criticizing the Executive. 'They' had missed God's will. We were not called to spend years with the Kenyah.

But what was all this sickness about? Was God trying to say something to us through it? Of course, when someone else is sick we should never say that it is because they have sinned, and that God is trying to get something through to them. But it may be appropriate in this sort of situation to examine ourselves and ask if the Lord is allowing a little loving 'chastening'. Whether the Executive was right or wrong was not the point at that stage. What was wrong was our attitude to them. Had we not agreed to honour our leaders and abide by their decisions? They were just as concerned as we were that we should be doing the Lord's will. Also, we believed fervently in the sovereignty of God. Could we not trust him to overrule, even if the Executive had made a mistake?

Having asked the Lord to forgive us, and re-affirming our confidence that he was in control, we pledged ourselves to apologize to the Executive when we next saw them. We were even open to the idea that God might want to convince us that we should be spending several years with the Kenyah. It was his prerogative to direct his forces in the best way possible. It was possible we had misunderstood his leading about the Tagals. It was also possible that this was another 'Abramic' experience. Were we being asked to express our willingness not to go to the Tagals but to leave the outcome to God? With this surrender of our own wills, we experienced a great sense of peace and forgiveness and an awareness that God could be trusted. And, though we did not know it at the time, just as with Abraham, God already had a solution worked out. It was most unexpected, and Ray would explain it to us on his return.

Meanwhile, on with the job

In the meantime, we got on with the job in hand, with Bill getting rapidly better from that moment onwards. But we were still anxious to know what had happened to Ray. We were running out of food. Would Ray be back before our supplies ran out completely?

'What's that? Listen!' We stood motionless to see if the noise would get louder. It was either a boat with an outboard engine coming up – or was it down – the river, or the aeroplane. We almost held our breath so as to hear more clearly.

'Oh, no,' I exclaimed, and could have cried. It was one of those horrible big black borer beetles making holes in the softwood timber of our little house.

Again and again we experienced the same momentary elation, only to be disappointed.

'It really is this time! The plane!' What a wonderful sound! We rushed outside to look. Of course it couldn't land but it was good to see it. It must be taking Ray to the airstrip upriver. He would arrive tomorrow. But then it began to circle. Once, twice, three times. We waved and then it dawned on us that the pilot was going to do an airdrop.

We had not been forgotten. In fact the members of the mission at headquarters had been extremely worried about these two raw recruits all alone in the far interior. Morning by morning at the prayer meeting, they had been praying for us. We really were quite a liability up there on our own. They were very anxious to know how we were. The pilot dropped a letter tied to a stone. It landed perfectly beside our house, right in the middle of the little jungle clearing which was used as a football field.

'Please light a smokey fire to show that you are ready for an airdrop,' it read, 'and wave your arms if you are all right.'

We scurried around to find something to burn. As there was no airstrip there, we were not like other interior missionaries, ready with the wherewithal to light a smokey fire. But it didn't take long. As the thick smoke rose from the damp grass, we waved our arms with great excitement.

The pilot couldn't drop supplies but he did drop a lovely big bag of mail – six weeks' accumulation, and an explanation of why Ray had not returned (or at least half an explanation: Ray would tell us the rest when we saw him). Ray had had to go on an even more urgent assignment nearer the coast and would be back in another three weeks. The mission team was very thin on the ground and a crisis had arisen in another area which needed immediate attention. The Executive had felt that Ray was the only one who could go. They had decided that they would have to trust the Lord to look after us but they wanted to make sure we were all right. We had not been forgotten. We waved acknowledgement. The pilot waggled the wings of the aircraft in reply and disappeared over the hills.

Jungle fish and chips

Three weeks! After our initial elation at seeing the
plane had died down, we began to wonder. Surely
there couldn't be a situation more urgent than ours!
Our supplies were desperately low. There must have
been someone else at headquarters who could have
gone. We were again tempted to be critical of the
Executive in delaying Ray's return. We had certainly
learnt to trust God to supply our financial needs, but
this was more immediate. For three weeks we were
going to have to trust him literally for our daily
bread – or rather rice!

A few days later we heard the rhythmic thud,
thud, thud of paddles clipping the side of a canoe. A
visitor? A medical problem perhaps. As Bill's medical skills had become known, we had frequent vis-
itors from all over the upper Baram area.

'The Education Officer is in the next village. He'll
be coming here tomorrow. He'd like to see you.'

We would have to give him a meal and possibly put
him up for the night.

'Lord, you know all about this. We cannot dishon-
our your name. Even if the Executive has again
slightly missed the point, your honour is at stake. It
will not be understood if we don't produce a decent
meal and the Mission will be criticized. Lord, you'll
have to do something. We can't give him a tin of pilchards' (that was about all we had left).

Do something he did. Not long after our prayer, a
local villager brought us a huge armful of *ubi kayu* ,
apologizing that it wasn't rice. *Ubi kayu* is a tapioca-

65

like plant which, when fried, makes the most delicious chips but it is only eaten by the Kenyah as a poor substitute for rice. In the circumstances, it was much better than rice. We had been given some wild pig fat earlier. But we had no meat. With a bit of bartering, we managed to persuade someone to go fishing. Next morning this man brought us two of the largest fish we'd ever seen in our time in the interior.

'God gave us a good catch!' was the comment from this man who was still a pagan. We had a lovely opportunity to explain to him about our prayer and our all-powerful God. We said a hearty thank-you to our benefactor and to the Lord. The man went away very thoughtful, and we entertained the English Government Officer to 'jungle fish and chips'. He loved it.

God was teaching us that we could trust him to look after us even when we felt we might be in that situation simply due to some not very good planning on behalf of our leaders.

Another's needs

We were praying that he would be doing the same for the young pastor and his wife living downriver. They were from the Lun Bawang tribe and were serving a Christian village a couple of hours away. They would be being tested as we were. They were very young and in many ways it had been a far bigger step of faith and commitment for them to leave their own tribe and travel to the Kenyah area, than it had been for us to leave England and go to Borneo. We had all lived together for our first few weeks in the area and I had helped Bill when he delivered their first baby. Used to a close-knit extended family, they must have been feeling particularly isolated in these early months of parenthood. We longed to see them.

One day they called to see us. They were certainly lonely. They too were short of supplies, although more used to living in the jungle than we were. We talked and prayed together and, encouraged, they felt able to return. We were thankful that the baby was well and healthy.

'Wouldn't it be nice to give them a little present before they go?' Bill suggested as I prepared a meal for them.

'Yes, a lovely idea,' I agreed. 'But what?' I queried, thinking of our dwindling supplies. They were only lasting out because we were constantly being given gifts of rice and fern tips.

'What about a tin of condensed milk?'

'Oh no, not that!' I protested. We had two tins left and it was the only sweet thing we had. 'Wouldn't a tin of pilchards be just as good?' I continued, knowing full well that a tin of condensed milk was a real luxury to the tribespeople. They also crave from time to time for something sweet.

I slipped into our tiny bedroom where we kept our box of supplies. Yes, there were two tins. There were two or three tins of pilchards, a couple of tins of cheese and a small quantity of dried milk. That was all. It had to last at least another two weeks. Surely the pilchards would do. We were quite likely to be given some more fish, so we would not miss a tin too badly. But I knew what they would really appreciate.

'Why, Lord?' I fell on my knees in a turmoil of resentment, anger, fear. 'What are we going to live on? How long does this have to go on? We've repented of our rebellion. Must you go on, Lord? I do trust you but...'

I picked up my *Daily Light* in the hope of finding some words of comfort. Instead I read the verses for that day (changed here to the NIV wording):

'Go and work in my vineyard, and I will pay you whatever is right... A generous man will prosper; and he who refreshes others will himself be refreshed... God is not unjust; he will not forget your work and the love you have shown him as you have helped his people and continue to help them... Whatever you did for one of the least of these brothers of mine, you did for me...'[1]

I knew what I had to do. But still I hesitated. Then my eyes wandered over to the opposite page for the evening reading. 'The eyes of the LORD range throughout the earth to strengthen those whose hearts are fully committed to him... When you lie down, you will not be afraid; when you lie down, your sleep will be sweet.'[2] Only when I had done what God wanted me to do, could I expect to experience his peace. I would not be able to sleep peacefully that night if I were not obedient.

I was able to smile a very genuine smile as I said goodbye. I thought of the pleasure that that tin of milk would bring to the pastor and his wife whom we had grown to love very dearly. What a real joy it was to give them something I so much wanted to keep for myself. How little pleasure we often get out of our routine giving in church, or a gift to missions or some needy cause, because we give out of our plenty.

'God loves a cheerful [literally a "hilarious"] giver'

[1] Matthew 20:4; Proverbs 11:25; Hebrews 6:10; Matthew 25:40.
[2] 2 Chronicles 16:9; Proverbs 3:24.

(2 Corinthians 9:7).

Little did I know at the time that that tin of milk, two weeks later, was going to be the Lord's provision to save me from being seriously ill.

An unexpected solution

We had been called to the pastor's village to a major medical case and asked to do some teaching as well. I suddenly found myself with an acute abdominal pain. Bill prodded me around and looked puzzled and a little worried.

'It must be a really acute peptic ulcer,' he said with some hesitation and reluctance in his voice. The hesitation was partly because it is not a common condition but more because he knew he had nothing suitable in his 'jungle' medical box. The common digestive troubles of the West were not a feature of Bornean sickness and we ourselves never seemed to suffer from them either.

Bill knew the possible serious consequences of not treating it. Milk was the answer. But we had finished our small supply and so had not brought any down-river with us. Very reluctantly he asked the pastor if he had any milk.

'Yes, I have the tin you gave us,' was the pastor's cheerful reply (and I wondered what struggles they went through to give it to us).

'We were saving it for a special occasion,' he added.

We were amazed that they had not yet eaten their treasured possession and felt terrible receiving it back again. But it was the only hope of relief for the pain and avoiding serious consequences. The first drink had a dramatic effect – thus confirming the diagnosis. By watering it down considerably, we were able to spin it out over a couple of days. The crisis was over. As the tin ran out, Ray arrived with a boatload of supplies – a plentiful supply of dried milk, of which I consumed pints and pints over the next week, and several tins of condensed milk which we shared with the pastor and his wife.

We had had over three months of battling with ourselves, our circumstances, the Mission and with God. God had gone on patiently teaching us and in the end showing us that he could be trusted because he was in full control. At each point of crisis, he had stepped in. He loved us. He loved our fellow missionaries, he loved the pastor and his wife, he loved the Kenyah. He would not let any of us be tempted above our ability (with his strengthening) to cope. He also wanted the Tagals to have their New Testament, for he loved them too. He had worked out a lovely solution to that problem. Ray had got engaged while he had been at headquarters. His wife-to-be, a graduate from Melbourne University, was a gifted linguist and well able to undertake the translation of a New Testament with some help from Ray. He would continue to travel and Evelyn would do the major part of the translation.

Six weeks later we flew out to our headquarters and, after an apology to the Executive and a short holiday, we were soon on our way to tackle another language. This time it was Tagal. This time, too, we were sure we were meant to be translating a New Testament for them. We were also delighted to know that, after an initial two months' stay with them, we would be going on leave early in order to teach at the Wycliffe Course in England.

To think about

1. Our attitude to the Executive was very serious as it would grieve the Holy Spirit (Ephesians 4:29–32). Are there currently problems in your relationship with others? What are you going to do about them?

2. What are the relationships between sin and sickness? See John 5:5–9, 14; 9:1–3; Hebrews 4:11.

Bookshelf

The message of Ruth: The Wings of Refuge, David Atkinson (IVP, The Bible Speaks Today series, 1983; UK and US editions).
One in The Bible Speaks Today series, all of which we would strongly recommend. *The Message of Ruth* strengthens our belief in the overruling love of God. 'God...revealed in Christ and attested in the Scriptures is there; he cares, he rules, he provides' writes David Atkinson in this sensitive exposition. He traces the story of one small family against the background of the chaotic days 'when the judges ruled' and we see God lovingly bringing them into his overall plan of salvation.

From Fear to Faith, D. Martyn Lloyd-Jones (IVP, 1953).
Habakkuk wonders whether God can possibly be in control, and so do we sometimes as we look at history. Dr Lloyd-Jones takes us through the prophecy of Habakkuk to see that God reigns and Habakkuk comes through to be able to rejoice *in the Lord*.

6

A health revolution

The scourge of pneumonia ● *The tip of an iceberg* ●
Daring to trust Jesus ● *A dramatic change*

Two scraggy, sickly women puffed and panted their
way up the notched log leading to our little leaf and
bamboo hut. Although the house was only six feet
off the ground one of them had had to stop half way
up the 'steps' to get her breath before stepping onto
our verandah. They squatted on the floor and
untied the sarongs slung over their shoulders.

'*Narualan, narualan bonsoi.* [Sick, very sick.]' they
said, dispensing with the normal lengthy courtesies
of a visit. They carefully laid their sarongs on the
floor and began to unfold several layers of clean but
old greying rags to reveal their tiny sick babies.

We were living in the village of Meligan in Tagal
country. The villagers had built us this house so that
we could live with them, learn the language, teach
them and translate a New Testament. We had not
been there many months, so language was still a
problem. But we knew 'narualan'. It was one of the
first words we had learnt as news of Bill's medical
skills had spread. The tribe was known by the Government and by the World Health Organization to
be dying out, partly from sickness but also from

sterility. The latter was mainly due to their promiscuity which had followed a Government ruling some years previously. They had decreed that the Tagals should no longer follow their custom of the death penalty for a man and woman involved in adultery. Such promiscuity had meant a rapid spread of a venereal infection which in turn had led to widespread sterility. We had seen this for ourselves some months earlier when travelling further afield and night-stopping in a village. There was one child three years of age and no-one else under the age of about twenty.

The scourge of pneumonia

Meligan was not as bad as that. There were some babies and a few children. Nevertheless, of those who were born, the majority had died in infancy or childhood, quite frequently of pneumonia. In fact, as Bill had seen one after another chronically or acutely ill men, women and children, he was coming to the conclusion that pneumonia, or its after effects, were the main causes of early death.

The pneumonia was quite easy to treat provided it was caught early enough and the response was quite dramatic. But was it the main problem? It seemed to be at first, as again and again it was the acute illness for which medical help was sought. They knew only too well that a full-grown person could be dead within twenty-four hours if they didn't get help. Why so soon?

Bill carefully examined the two babies, though it did not take him long to see that they too had pneumonia. They lived nearby so they had come

73

soon enough for him to cure them, but he knew full well that they could well succumb again in a few months. Was he to spend years fighting such a rearguard action? The babies were incredibly anaemic, and he noticed that the mothers were too, although they were not asking for medicine for themselves. He began to examine them, explaining, through interpretation, that he thought their sickness might be affecting the babies. He pulled down the lower eyelid of one of the women. It was almost dead white. The palms of her hands were too. Although Bill could not measure the haemoglobin levels in such a remote area, his previous experience in a Government hospital in Malaya told him it was likely to be around twenty-five per cent of what it should be. In Malaya he had become accustomed to patients coming into hospital with such dreadfully low haemoglobin levels. When the patients had reached fifty per cent of normal levels, they had felt so well, that they wanted to go home.

'Stay a little longer, and I can get you really well,' he had often almost pleaded with the patients.

'No, thank you. We must get back to the farm. You've cured us. We've never felt so well in all our lives.'

And off they had gone with a level of haemoglobin which would have put us, in the developed world, *into* hospital on a stretcher.

The tip of an iceberg

As Bill looked at these two women and the babies in their arms, he was faced with a dilemma. He was beginning to see them as the tip of the proverbial

74

iceberg. How should he respond in the face of the total situation? Even if there had been a hospital nearer than five days' walk away, he could not put the whole population into it. He could give everyone a course of iron pills, or even an injection of iron, and the results could well have been dramatic.

There was a real difficulty with that solution to the problem. If the Tagals came to think that the only way to feel well was to have iron pills, what would happen if we were not there? They could become dependent on traders nearer the coast.

Having dealt with the acute symptoms of pneumonia in the two babies, Bill decided to try a 'jungle' cure for the anaemia in the two mothers. He was looking for a dietetic revolution that would change the health of the Tagals and greatly increase their resistance to disease.

'I want you to eat vegetables three times a day and then come and see me in a month's time,' he suggested. He was well aware that the lush jungle provided them with plenty of iron-rich vegetables.

'We can't do that,' they said almost in unison. 'We'll die.'

Bill was prepared for resistance, but why this terrified look on their faces? They really meant it when they said they thought they would die. Only eighteen months previously they had turned to Christianity from their animism – fear of the power of evil spirits. What we did not know at that stage was that, under their old custom, no pregnant or lactating woman was allowed to eat vegetables. And vegetables were the main source of the iron so much needed during pregnancy. They feared terrible reprisals from the spirits if they disobeyed. How hideously cruel the enemy is. He not only holds men and women in spiritual darkness, he is determined to ruin their bodies as well. It had been a great step of faith for these Tagals to turn away from so powerful an enemy and to believe that Jesus was victorious. In the last eighteen months they had been proving this fact daily as they disobeyed the messages from the spirits – messages which used to keep them from guarding their farms near harvest time. 'It's better to starve than risk offending the spirits,' they used to say. But they had disobeyed them and prayed to Jesus for protection, and he had kept them safe.

Daring to trust Jesus

Here however was a very different sort of disobedience. It was more personal. It might mean the death of their babies. Could they trust this white man? Bill sought the pastor's help. Amat was from the neighbouring Lun Bawang tribe, and he was the one who had first shared the gospel with them in spite of his natural fears of going to his former head-hunting enemies. He'd lived with them for eighteen months and the people were well aware that things had certainly been better since they had followed Jesus. Amat reminded these women what they had learnt about the Lord Jesus Christ. He told them again of Christ's power, of his love for them, of his dying for them and his total triumph over Satan. He prayed with them and fearfully but hopefully they began to nod agreement.

'But we'll get sick tummies. We are not used to vegetables,' they protested as a last-ditch resistance.

'If you get sick tummies, I'll treat the sickness,' Bill

promised them.

They collected up their little bundles, slung them once more across their backs and made their way slowly down the notched log. We watched them go, praying that God would give them courage. Bill turned to Amat.

'Would you come with me to the native chief, please? I would like you to help me to explain to him how important it is that these women do what I have told them to.'

The native chief responded warmly and promised to make sure that the families knew what was to be done, and he personally would keep a check. In this way the eating of green vegetables became a much talked-about village 'event'. It also soon became apparent to everyone that, not only were the babies recovering after their treatment, but the women, without medicine, were getting better. The two women had become celebrities and a little crowd followed them when they revisited us a month later. They almost ran up the notched log. Their babies were looking alert. The mothers had lost the awareness of their hearts beating heavily. Their eyelids were beginning to look pink. They knew they were much better.

Other women in the village began to follow their example and they too were astonished how much better they felt. And they all talked about it. Their pagan neighbours were becoming very curious. Soon we saw a very practical example of the church being 'the salt of the earth'. Pagan social sanctions were being broken into. The enemy was forced to back off and the pagan leaders found ways of sanctioning the eating of vegetables, lest the people's envy of the health of the Christians should precipitate a rush to change their faith. The 'roaring lion' had to modify his tactics, but he didn't disappear. He became an 'angel of light'.

A dramatic change

The overall health of the community at Meligan improved rapidly. Pneumonia became much less common as their stronger bodies were better able to resist the disease. But this had only been possible initially because first they had been freed from the enslaving power of animism. The gospel had also brought the incentive and ability to turn from drunkenness and promiscuity, with the result that growing girls and young mums were no longer becoming sterile. More babies were born. Fewer babies and small children died. In fact, within just ten years, there was another problem.

'Rangai [my Bornean name], how is it that you have been here ten years and yet you still have only three children?' I was asked one day by a 'delegation' of lay leaders from the village to which we had then moved.

'Our wives', they continued, 'are having so many children that they are *rosak*.' They used a word which they borrowed from Malay, which is usually used for a piece of machinery which has broken down, rather than their word for 'sick'. 'We used to be worried that we had so few children and so many died. Now we are having too many and most of them are living.' Fortunately there was a major Government centre just a day's walk away and the doctor at the hospital had started a family planning clinic. We suggested that they should give him a visit.

A Christian community had opened the way to the possibility of a dietetic revolution which had led to a health revolution. In just ten years, instead of the majority of babies dying, the majority lived. God had given the vision to see that preventative not curative medicine was the primary responsibility of a doctor in an isolated 'undoctored' situation. But it was obvious that such a programme could only be carried out as the church was established. Men and women learnt to know and experience that Jesus is Victor and that they do not need to fear the spirits. Bill was convinced that, in spite of the appalling amount of illness, God's direction for him was an emphasis on Bible teaching and preventative medicine rather than curative medicine.

He was, in fact, not a medical missionary in the popular understanding of that word.

'If God had called me to medical work as my primary responsibility,' he explained over and over again to those mystified by his lack of zeal for building a hospital, 'then I would have worked in a Government hospital as I did in Malaya. But God has the prerogative to lead me into a medical career and then to lead me out of primary emphasis on medicine into a work of Bible teaching and church planting. I do medical work that comes to hand to demonstrate the love of Christ and to help these sick people. But that is not my primary responsibility when God has called me to establish a church.'

Bill had assumed there would be a major health 'spin-off' but confessed to being amazed by the total impact. While he treated all who came to him, and any he met on his travels, he did not specifically spend long hours trekking to find the sick. This led to some misunderstanding with the Government.

'What's that mad doctor doing up there in the interior?' was the question asked by a somewhat irate District Officer on one occasion.

It took ten years for the health revolution to begin to convince them that his policy in Tagal country was paying off. And now some thirty years after our first visit the situation is quite staggering. When we returned to the area in 1984, we were met by 150 people from Meligan who had travelled to the convention nearest to their village.

'Do you remember giving me medicine when I was a baby at Meligan?' was a question from some of the healthiest young mums we have ever seen in Tagal country. And the teenagers, whose childhood years had been most affected by the new dietary habits of their parents, are fit, healthy and sturdy (and three inches taller). A senior Malaysian Government Officer whom we had known as a clerk in those early days greeted us warmly. How different were his comments from the former Government Officer.

There is an acute medical need in many parts of the world, and we owe it to our fellow men and women to help them. Christian medical students and doctors, when considering how God can use them, will obviously consider the alleviation of suffering in any part of the world. Many will be led to serve God in medical work in Government or existing missionary hospitals. But we all need to beware of dictating to God that, because he has led us into a certain area of training, he has to lead us to continue in that area. This is a particular danger for medical students. He may call any of us into a church-planting, Bible-teaching ministry. For a doctor or nurse, their medical skills will then be used in a secondary capacity, especially in situations where the density of population cannot possibly support the building of a hospital. While being involved in a church-planting ministry, they will obviously treat the sick, but it will be as a demonstration of the love and compassion of Christ, not their primary role. However, within that context, they may well find that they can have a greater effect on the health of the people through a preventative medical programme than if they had been primarily in a healing ministry in a hospital.

To think about

1. Jesus went about 'teaching, preaching and healing', but did he heal everyone in Palestine in his day? Put as a contemporary question, does God look to his *church* (as opposed to individual Christians) to run a health service? Look at Matthew 4:23–25; 14:13–14; Luke 4:40–44; 7:20–23; Matthew 13:53–58.
   What was Jesus' *primary* aim? See Luke 19:10; John 6:38–40.

2. When Jesus sent out his disciples, what did he tell them to do? See Luke 9:1–6.

3. Did Jesus care for his disciples' well-being as well as the multitudes? See Mark 6:30–34.

Bookshelf

Mister Leprosy, Phyllis Thompson (Hodder and Stoughton and the Leprosy Mission, 1980).
'Mr Leprosy' is Dr Stanley Browne, who was one of

the most able doctors of our time. His great break-through, on the very early diagnosis of leprosy, which made him world famous, was greatly aided by his excellent working relationship with the local Africans from whom he learnt much.

Kanchi Doctor – Ruth Watson of Nepal, David Hawker (Scripture Union, 1984).
A very human story of a close friend of ours, a single lady doctor who shared in pioneering medical work in the remote hills of Nepal. Medical work was the only way of access into this closed country but Ruth, though an extremely gifted and dedicated doctor, was never to be confined to medical work. The establishment of the church in the Pokhara valley bears testimony to that.

As she wrote her last letter to her Nepali friends before her death from a brain tumour in 1976 at the age of fifty, she shows this clearly:

'...it is this love of God that I long to share with you in Pokhara. You know that is why I really came to Pokhara, not just to minister to sick bodies, but to help you to understand that God loves you...so much that he gave his son...to die for you. And as I wait these last few weeks here on earth, my one prayer is that in Nepal many, many will come to know this wonderful truth.'

Don't just stand there..., Martin Goldsmith (IVP, 1976; now jointly published with STL).
Chapter 8, 'Hey you with two coats!', gives a most helpful look at the dilemmas of medicine in missions.

A pastor preaching from newly translated New Testament.

Kenyah woman, from the Baram, doing beadwork.

Bill and Ruth going for a bath in the river at Meligan. Ruth is 20 months old here.

First Kenyah pastor and his wife.

Amat and family.

A pastor harvesting in Sabah.

The bazaar at Lawas (downriver from Mission headquarters).

Meligan pastor hunting with a blowpipe.

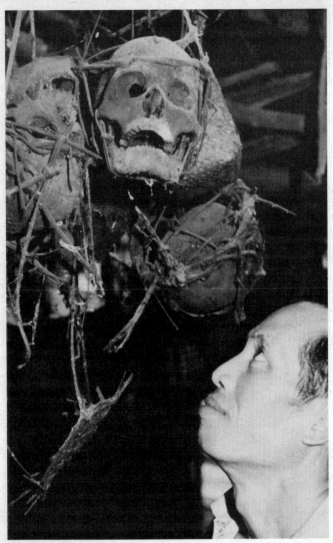

No longer head-hunters, but skulls were kept.

'. . . all that was needed was a quick, deft stroke with his jungle knife' (chapter 1).

7

Planned withdrawal

Stifling growth ● *Encouraging the local church* ●
Completing the task ● *Rebellion* ● *Bill returns – and
reports* ● *God's timing*

Missionaries can stay too long! This was Bill's conclusion by the time he left Malaya. At that stage he was a 'non-professional' missionary in a Government hospital. After being 'professional' missionaries for fourteen years, it's a view we still hold.

Although Bill was in Malaya on a short-term contract with the Government Medical Service, he preached regularly at weekends, sometimes as many as five times. He shared with the missionaries in outreach and Bible teaching. But being on the 'outside' he had an opportunity to see 'the wood for the trees'. He thought a great deal about the ultimate aim of missions because he was not snowed under with the business of the everyday ministries. He thought about the great master missionary Paul, who could state, 'Now...there is no more place for me to work in these regions' (Romans 15:23). This did not seem to be the basic pattern of modern missions as he looked at the situations around him. Wonderfully devoted, able and godly missionaries seemed to feel called to stay where they were for life, even though the church was well-established.

Stifling growth

These missionaries were certainly leading to Christ men and women. Gifted Bible teachers, they were also very caring. They were, however, so competent in every way that it was difficult for them to think of handing over any responsibility to those who, initially, would not do the job as well as they did it themselves. The gifts of these new Christians were inevitably hindered from developing by the very presence of the missionaries.

'They are so concerned about the lack of local leadership,' Bill had commented to me on his return to England. 'I don't think they can see that it might be they who are inhibiting it. Yet who am I to criticize? They have such a marvellous concern for the Lord's work. Their devotion to the Lord puts me to shame.'

Bill was beginning to see the urgent need for missions to think about giving space and opportunity for the local church, and particularly the leadership, to grow and develop. In order to achieve this, withdrawal must be planned. The initial thinking about a new outreach must include clear ideas about the completion of the Mission's contribution. But the idea that missionaries should actually think of finishing their task and moving on was rather revolutionary in the 1950s, in spite of the recent enforced withdrawal of the whole missionary enterprise from China. The unwritten ethos of missions was still to think of enlisting for life, and that missionaries who left the 'land of their adoption' and returned home were failures – almost by definition!

A commitment for life to any particular task however encourages the idea that there is plenty of time.

This leads to a disastrous delay in the development of God-given local leadership.

'I'm committed to the Lord for life,' Bill explained to one of his critics who thought he was sheltering behind these thoughts because he did not want to make a life-long commitment to a mission.

'I'm not necessarily committed to a particular mission for life,' he continued. 'God is the "I am" – the God of the present, the living God. We cannot say to him "You led me into medicine. You cannot lead me into Bible teaching" any more than we can say "You led me to Borneo. You cannot lead me anywhere else or even home again." '

Encouraging the local church

It was therefore exciting to get involved with a mission like the BEM. It had always been committed to an 'indigenous policy'. The aim was to produce a self-supporting, self-governing, self-propagating church as soon as possible. Local leadership was trained and encouraged immediately there were a few Christians. As village after village became Christians, the people were encouraged to build their own church and pastor's house and work towards supporting their own pastor. In 1950 an even bolder step was taken. The Governing Field Conference considered a suggestion from the home end that they should adopt a ten-year plan for the completion of the work of establishing the church.

They were a small team of young and mostly inexperienced missionaries. Only six of the pre-war team had been able to return to Borneo when peace came, and two of those had soon had to go home.

Too high a proportion of them were still at the language-learning stage. The churches were in need of the translation of Bibles or at least New Testaments into their own languages. The medical needs were immense – sickness and malnutrition were major problems. Illiteracy needed to be tackled. The Bible School had been opened only four years previously.

Courageously, nevertheless, they took a step of faith, believing the suggestion to be from the Lord. After prayer and discussion they decided they needed fifteen years if they were going to produce a New Testament for each of the yet-unwritten language groups, in some of which no-one had even started learning the language. The fifteen-year plan was adopted. This was later changed to a fifteen-year policy to allow for advance into other areas. As each successive tribe was entered, the team should pray for, plan for and work for the completion of the task in the next fifteen years.

The mission set a prayer target of twelve new missionaries in the next twelve months – a seventy per cent increase in the team! God put his seal on the plan by providing the twelve within that time, most of whom had actually reached Borneo by the time of the next Field Conference in 1952. We were two of them and we arrived just a few weeks before the conference.

Completing the task

Of course as new recruits we were not eligible to take part in the discussions, though the most senior missionary had suggested that we all be allowed to observe. It became obvious that some of the missionaries were still a bit bewildered by their decision of two years previously, and didn't really know what it involved. Bill was asked to give a paper on the subject, based on what he had learnt in Malaya. He shared the great burden he had to see missions with an aim to complete their task and hand over to the local church. A fresh enthusiasm for the policy was the result, and we marvelled at the privilege of being involved with a Mission which was not only prepared to be adventurous in its policies, but willing to listen to the burden and vision the Lord had given to one of its most recent recruits.

When we came home on our first leave, we had an exciting message for the churches and student groups to whom we spoke. The BEM became widely known as the mission with a fifteen-year policy – a mission that was prepared to think of working itself out of a job. It was a young mission and it appealed to those who wanted to see missions keep moving in the task of world evangelism. But was it *too* young? Were we irresponsible and was the policy just a gimmick to free us from a commitment for life? Did it really have a sound biblical basis?

Bill wrote a series of articles for the Christian press which some years later were put into booklet form by the Overcomer Literature Trust under the title *Second Thoughts on Missions*. The following extracts on our need to rethink our expectations of what God will do amongst new Christians, are perhaps as relevant today as they were then.

God's gifts

'God has planned specific provision for the building up of the body (the church) through the giving of the gifts of the Spirit (1 Corinthians 12; Ephesians

94

4). He makes adequate provision for his church. We must pray for these promised gifts to the new churches. Perhaps more important, we should pray that we shall recognize them as God gives them. The gift of the pastor may be found in a Penan jungle nomad. The fact that he picks his way through trackless areas of primary tropical Bornean jungle in nothing but a bark loincloth, armed with poisoned darts and blowpipe, must not put us off. Nor must we allow ourselves to be deceived by a non-Western temperament.

'As an average missionary, I am learning to expect that God will raise up some of my tribal brethren to be my betters as preachers and teachers. God gives his gifts "according to their several abilities". He does it adequately, indeed lavishly. It is my firm conviction that whether or not the gifts develop depends on the attitude and the expectation of those of us called to pray and work among them.'

Evangelism
'As the result of new believers' witness it was not long before there was a daughter church springing up three days' walk away from the village we were visiting. We noted that the pastor's question to those returning from visits to relatives, or from work nearer the coast, was full of significance. It was not, "Did you have an opportunity to witness?" but "What was the response when you spoke about the Lord?" The choice of question was a clear indication of his belief and confidence in the indwelling Holy Spirit, whose nature and commission had not changed. He was and is the one who specifically empowers believers to be witnesses to the Saviour (Acts 1:8).'

Scaffolding

'The essential character of a builder or contractor is his clarity of thought about the finished product. He will use many devices and much scaffolding to achieve his purpose; but the means will never be such as will damage the building... It is unthinkable that any constructor would produce a house propped up by scaffolding. What a house it would be if it began to totter as he removed what was meant to be a temporary aid to construction.

'Missionaries are God's scaffolding, used as he builds his church in new areas. He does not intend that they should be props to the building... There is however a complicating factor. God's scaffolding is animated and always anxious to be helpful. During construction some parts of the building may seem to be inadequate. We tend to respond to this situation by becoming part of the structure ourselves. Is this due to an inability to understand the adequacy of the unseen strengthening features? Or is it an unrecognized lack of confidence in the Designer?'

Independence

'Our problem is to go on helping new churches like an intelligent parent with a little child. Parents have to be ready to take risks of infection and accident or else pamper and spoil. They have to risk falls or delay development. We too have to take risks.'

Withdrawal

'When Jesus Christ called the twelve, he announced his plan of campaign. He was going to train them, hand over to them and leave them. The great commission to world evangelism was not an afterthought. It was clearly uppermost in his mind as he called the disciples. With his call he gave a summary of his plan. "Come, follow me, and I will make you fishers of men" (Mark 1:17). The material he had was not exactly promising. His relationship to and confidence in his Father and in the Holy Spirit enabled him to endure the heartbreak of many defections and the slowness of heart of those the Father had specifically given to him. Here surely is the key to understanding his completed task of preparing the disciples to evangelize the world. He had God's plan. He planned withdrawal before he started. He knew where he was going. Yet the crucial thing was the relationship rather than the strategy.'

The fifteen-year policy was founded on biblical principles. We were motivated by the thought of trying to follow the Lord's and Paul's examples. However, the church was growing fast - almost too fast. We were all busy. There was so much to do. We began to get bogged down in the day-to-day business and to lose our sense of the 'finishability' of our task. Whereas for the first ten years the fifteen-year policy was constantly being referred to, very subtly we began to forget about it or rationalize it. Time seemed to be on our side. Year by year we were getting more and more comfortably and permanently established at our headquarters in Lawas.

Rebellion

Then suddenly it happened. Twelve years after the formation of the fifteen-year policy, the Brunei Rebellion jolted us out of our complacency... One day we were an oasis of peace in south-east Asia. The next day, Europeans were being used as human shields as the 'rebels' attacked Government offices and tried to take over the country. Life itself suddenly became less secure. Death was a real possibility. What would happen to the church if we were all killed? Material things became less important. The future became very uncertain.

In the mercy of God, our local District Officer had been alerted to what was happening a week before and he had rounded up all the ring leaders in the area. But nevertheless we waited all night, quite defenceless, in houses which didn't even have locks on the outside doors.

The next day it was decided we should move out to the island of Labuan. A large group of Europeans was too much of a liability for the local government. The little plane flew in and out all day. The older children (including our second daughter, Heather) were safely at school in Kota Kinabalu in Sabah but there were still more than enough passengers. We sent our next daughter Val off on the last trip with our good friends the pilot and his wife when it became obvious that there were not enough daylight hours for us all to go. Bill was acting chairman at the time and so it was obvious that we would be the ones to stay behind.

We spent the night in a Lun Bawang longhouse, not knowing whether it would be our last on earth, but we had real peace and a sense that God was allowing this for his purposes. I remember reading that night:

'You will go out in joy and be led forth in peace; the mountains and hills will burst into song before you... Instead of the thornbush will grow the pine tree, and instead of briers the myrtle will grow. This will be for the LORD's renown...' (Isaiah 55:12–13).

Bill returns – and reports

Next morning we flew out, but Bill returned two days later. He got permission to go and live with the District Officer and other officials in the Government offices, which had been turned into a fort. They would not allow him back onto the mission site, but he was able to keep in touch with the church and Bible School staff and students. His movements were very restricted and in the comparative inactivity of his confinement, he was already beginning to think. He had been told by the Chairman, before he had gone on leave, that he was not to think of his time in office as a 'caretaker government'. He was free to think new thoughts if the situation demanded it.

Why had God allowed this? It began to look as if he was giving us a reminder that we were not to be there for life. Twelve of the fifteen years had gone and we didn't seem to have made any positive steps towards withdrawal of the Mission from the church base. Bill began to think that one of the best ways of encouraging independence in the church would be to distance the Mission headquarters from the central base of the church (now officially known as the Sidang Injil Borneo, that is 'the evangelical church of Borneo'). This would entail moving from Lawas. Not only would that mean that the SIB leadership would then be free to lead in their own way. If we moved to the coastal town of Miri where a church was already growing, it would also mean having a good base from which to take up the amazing new opportunities in the towns.

A week later, when we had all returned to a somewhat uneasy peace, he spent several days with the

Executive Committee in thinking, praying and discussion. The Mission was at a crossroads. They had to decide what God was saying through the upheaval of the Rebellion. Were we to carry on with our principal orientation towards the interior, but with renewed vision for the fifteen-year policy? Or should we be thinking of making some sort of move towards the towns?

Bill wrote up the Executive's findings, which were warmly received by those in Borneo who had experienced the Rebellion. The exploratory nature of the paper, however, was misunderstood by several of those on leave in Australia who felt that the Executive had over-reacted and gone ahead without consultation. Bill apologized and withdrew the paper, but it was too late. The Mission was divided. We all continued to work together but there were underlying tensions. It took twelve years before there was sufficient healing in the Mission for the next generation of leaders to complete the move to Miri.

Those of us on both sides of the disagreement felt battered and bruised. In some ways it was fortunate that we had to come home three years later. In England, God gave us new spheres in which to share ideas and vision, and a few years later we experienced the real joy of restored relationships. Meeting up again with those involved, we were once more able to enjoy the fun, friendship and fellowship that we had known in earlier years.

God's timing

It had taken a long time and this was a very sad

period. There is however such an important lesson to be learnt that we feel we must include it. 'Young men in a hurry' both then and now may create problems. Their vision may be just what is needed. But vision that is inappropriately presented and pushed can split churches and can bring a nightmare of broken relationships both between individuals and churches. God's timing is so often not ours.

'With the Lord a day is like a thousand years, and a thousand years are like a day' (2 Peter 3:8).

Sometimes God seems to be doing so much all at once, that we can't keep up.

'Lord, there's too much happening,' we wanted to shout when the Tagal church was growing so fast. 'How do you expect us to feed all these young Christians?'

The consequences made us wonder why God did it.[1] But it certainly kept us aware of our limitations, and therefore increased our dependence on him.

At other times, the Lord seems to be moving so slowly and we wonder why he is so patient. But if he were not so patient, where would each of us be? When we feel like that now we constantly remind ourselves of how patient the Lord has been with us. There are things in our lives which he must long that we would change but he does not ride roughshod over us when we take years to do so.

Some months after the Brunei Rebellion, the Federation of Malaysia was formed in August 1963. Soon the Government announced that all ex-patriate missionaries should leave within quite a short period of time. The churches of Sabah and Sarawak spoke with a united voice. Anglicans, Baptists, the

---

[1] See chapter 10, 'Disciple-making and disappointments'.

101

Basel Mission, Methodists, Roman Catholics, Seventh Day Adventists and the SIB all claimed the freedom of religion as written into the Constitution, and asked for their missionaries to be allowed to stay. The Government agreed, but soon brought in their own ten-year policy. No ex-patriate missionary would be allowed to stay more than ten years. The missionary force of the BEM was soon to dwindle to a handful.

Ten years after the formation of Malaysia God showed how in his own way he was preparing his church for the years ahead. Between 1973 and 1974 he visited some groups of churches with revival, and what we could not do with our policies, however God-given, God himself began to do by his own power. Local leaders experienced an anointing from the Spirit, and churches were united in fellowship and in a renewed sense of responsibility for evangelism.

To think about

1. How patient are we? God is amazingly patient with us. Reflect on situations in your life where God has been patient with you. Look at Ephesians 4:30 to 5:2.

2. All of us will be involved with new Christians. What has this chapter to say to us (a) with regard to our expectations? (b) concerning our preparedness to take risks? (Think of a mother teaching a child to walk.)

Bookshelf

Drunk Before Dawn, Shirley Lees (OMF Books, 1979). Particularly read the chapters on 'Independence' and 'Revival'.

Missionary Methods: St Paul's or Ours? and *The Spontaneous Expansion of the Church*, Roland Allen (Eerdmans, 1962) are both well worth reading.

Written at the turn of the century, these books lay dormant for many years. Now reprinted, they are important reading for those seeking a right attitude towards missionary work, especially church-planting.

Don't just stand there..., Martin Goldsmith (IVP, 1976; now jointly published with STL).
A stimulating book which will help you to think through mission strategy and the Bible's teaching on mission. This teaching applies to God's church world-wide. As we plant churches, and encourage evangelism and leadership on the basis of God-given gifts, we should not neglect to encourage missionary vision in new as well as more established churches. A must for all with world-wide concern.

8

Special experiences and revival

Faith in decline • Singa's double grief •
A living example • Experiencing God • God's closeness •
Individuals in unity • Gifts — and the giver • Testing the
spirits • Of thumb-nails and rams

Long before the revival of 1974, the Bornean church had experienced various visitations of God's Spirit. Only a sovereign work of God could have turned the most degraded tribe in Borneo, the Lun Bawang (written up in the Government Gazette as being drunk a hundred days out of every 365) into the central group in the emergence of the evangelical church in Borneo. That was before the Japanese occupation. Only a further working of God's Spirit could have brought village after village of other tribespeople in Sarawak and Sabah from their total slavery to the spirits to freedom through Christ during the immediate post-war years.[1]

Not all had become born-again believers, but they had done what seemed impossible. They had turned their backs on the spirits and, in a courageous step of faith, had come to trust that Jesus was stronger than Satan. They were living in close-knit communities and they turned to believe in Christ for

[1] See Part 2, 'Daybreak' in *Drunk Before Dawn*, Shirley Lees (OMF, 1979).

deliverance as groups – 'mass conversion with regeneration in some and leading to regeneration in others', as one of the founder missionaries described it.

Faith in decline

God had worked amazingly, but even as early as 1950, there were already major problems of nominalism and legalism. The alcoholic Lun Bawang people had given up drink completely when they had become Christians. A Christian therefore did not drink. The reverse then became – if you drank you were not a Christian. And many who had given up drink along with the rest, but who had not come to personal faith, thought that they must be Christians because they didn't drink. This was a far cry from the vibrant Christianity of the early days of their defiance of the spirits.

The Chairman and his wife, Alan and Madge Belcher, began to be deeply concerned that such a church would not stand persecution. If all the missionaries were thrown out of Borneo, as they had recently been out of China, how would the church survive? They set themselves to pray with a new urgency, and to seek the Lord in renewal for themselves. Just before the 1952 Mission conference God had met with them in a new and life-changing way. Ripples of new blessing had spread as they shared their experience with the Lun Bawang, with whom they had been living in the interior of the northern part of Sarawak. After the conference, they shared what had happened with those in Bible School at Lawas. There was a new hunger for the Lord.

We were working on language analysis one afternoon and were suddenly disturbed by shouting and a lot of people running in different directions.

'Singa's little boy has disappeared!' we heard someone shout. Search-parties went out in several directions. They searched all night while others went to comfort the distraught parents.

'The spirits must have taken him.' Some were already wailing his death. Paganism was only just below the surface in some minds and they knew that no-one came back if the spirits had attacked. This made us missionaries pray all the harder that the little boy would be found. Our prayers had a very real but sad answer the next day. The party which had gone downriver returned with the little body, drowned in the deep-flowing Lawas river. The body had been washed up on the river bank several miles downstream. The grief was intense, but there was also a sense of thankfulness that, miraculously, the child's body had been found and had not been taken by alligators.

Singa

Singa was the head student of the Bible School. He'd been working as a pastor, having been to the little village Bible School run by the BEM missionaries before the war. He had come in for a refresher course. He was unusually tall for his generation of Lun Bawang. He was fit and strong too. He had been a Christian from his early teens, so that his did not show the ravages of malnutrition and of most of his tribe. With his unusual strong physique, he was also uncharacteristically proud. The Lun Bawang are normally a gentle, humble people.

Through his seemingly unconsolable grief, God spoke to Singa, both comforting him and bringing him into a new and deeper relationship with himself. As he came closer to his holy God, so he saw something of his own sin. Through tears of grief, as well as tears of repentance, he confessed to the sin of pride before his fellow students. God used his testimony and the shock of this tragedy to spark off a mini-revival in the school. This quickly spread to the Pastors' conference which met a few weeks later, and then to the conference for lay leaders from all over the Fifth Division of Sarawak. Each leader came under deep conviction of sin and, with their repentance and forgiveness, God gave a new vitality to their faith. As they returned to their villages on fire for the Lord, so the churches were re-kindled. God also stimulated a new hunger for the Lord in the missionary team, and one by one, over the next few months, we too experienced the same conviction of sin, repentance, forgiveness and renewal. Each entered into a new joy, a new desire for his Word and for prayer and a new zeal for his work.

A living example

We had the privilege of living with the Belchers during part of this period. We have often said as we look back on those days that they preached an extraordinarily high standard of Christian living and yet lived above it themselves. They talked freely of their experiences and of their communion with the Lord. We marvelled at the time (and even more in retrospect) at the *way* in which they shared 'the deep things of God' with us. They talked so naturally and lovingly, as if we understood all that they were sharing with us. They never gave the impression of superior knowledge or experience. They never made us feel 'second class', as so often happens when Christians have had an exciting new experience of the Lord. They never once suggested that we should have their experience, or that we were in any way lacking in our Christian lives. The more we shared with them, the deeper our love and respect for them grew, and the more we realized that we did not have their warmth of fellowship with the Lord. We longed to enter into the reality of such a relationship. We began to ask the Lord to meet us.

Bill went off into Tagal country with two Lun Bawang pastors. This involved three weeks of walking, preaching the gospel to those who had not yet heard, and surveying the area to see where God was wanting us to work. While away, the Lord met with him.

'My sense of sin was overwhelming,' he explained later. He had sought the Lord in repentance and had experienced such a sense of forgiveness and joy in his presence, that he had really begun to wonder whether he had been a Christian before. Of course he knew he had been. But there was now a whole new dimension to his life.

I knew nothing of this at the time because there was no means of communication from the interior of Tagal country. He had given us a date when he hoped to be back, but he didn't arrive. Twenty-four hours later he still had not returned. I began to think the worst.

Experiencing God

God used my worry and my distress to bring me to my knees. The Belchers had been talking over lunch about Luke 11. 'If your son asks for a fish, will [you] give him a snake instead?' (verse 11). I had spoken about the dangers of counterfeit experience and Alan had told me how the Chinese can cook snake in such a way that you would be convinced that it is fish. He had then gone on to insist that God will not give counterfeits to his children, even if it is almost unrecognizable as not being the real thing. He finished up with verse 13: 'If you then, though you are evil, know how to give good gifts to your children, how much more will your Father in heaven give the Holy Spirit to those who ask him!'

I knew I had God's Spirit in my life but I had been so afraid of the counterfeit that I was afraid to ask him to fill me. I thought back to the days when I was a student and the 'second blessing' teaching was going around the universities. I had had a number of conversations with a friend about it. I came out of church one Sunday morning after the sermon had filled my heart with a longing to know more of the Lord. The preacher hadn't divided Christians into the 'haves' and 'have nots' as some speakers seemed to be doing. He just gave us a longing to know more of the Lord's working in our lives. I'd asked the Lord at the end of the service to show me how to 'grow in the grace and knowledge of...Christ' (2 Peter 3:18).

I met this friend on the steps and commented on the hunger in my heart. He immediately interpreted that as a desire for the 'second blessing' experience. He spoke about a girl we both knew. 'You can see from her eyes that she has received it,' he commented.

'What do you mean?' I asked, and he tried for about the fourth time to persuade me that I needed a second blessing. I was resistant. Finally in loving exasperation he said, 'I can't help you any more Shirley. You will just have to go home and wait for it.'

It. I didn't want it, whatever it was. I wanted *him.* I didn't want any short cuts to maturity, nor did I want anything counterfeit. I knew this friend's experience was real, but some of the students I knew seemed to me to have worked up an experience in order not to feel inferior, but it didn't seem to make any difference to their Christian living. I didn't blame them. The pressure was often quite strong, but I didn't want an experience for experience sake. So I turned my back on this 'blessing'.

Here I was faced with a not dissimilar situation. But this time I was desperate. I had argued myself into thinking that the Lord would delay Bill from getting home until I had got myself straightened out, so I had to do something and do it quickly. I asked the Lord to forgive me for my hardness of heart and for various other attitudes, especially my ulterior motives. God began to show me my sinful nature and I wept in repentance. I asked him to fill me with his Spirit and to keep his promise that he would not give me a 'snake for a fish'. He answered my prayer and filled me with a wonderful sense of forgiveness, cleansing and joy.

Just a few hours later, Bill walked in. We shared our experiences and rejoiced together that God had blessed us similarly although separated by many miles. From then on we both knew a joy and excitement in serving the Lord which we had not known before. In particular we had a wonderful delight in studying his Word. He daily gave us new insights as we read the Bible.

God's closeness

It was not long before we went off to spend some time at Meligan. We saw God working and answering prayer but the biggest change we experienced was the sense of fellowship with the Lord in our 'quiet times'. On our next visit to Lawas, when our turns came round to lead the prayer meeting, we shared some of the understandings that God had been giving us from his Word.

'What's happened to you two?' one of our fellow missionaries queried after a few weeks. 'Every time you take the prayer meeting the Lord speaks to my heart.'

We were rather surprised. We didn't really think we were doing more than explaining the passages we had read, though of course we knew that God had spoken to us first. This had given a reality to what we were saying. We were sharing the Word, as the Belchers had done with us, but we prayed that we would never make anyone feel they were inferior.

As one and another moved into a new relationship with the Lord in various ways, our hearts were filled with love for one another. They were exciting days. When Bill and I came home on leave after two years in Borneo (we came home early to teach at the Wycliffe course), we longed to get back to our friends in Lawas. We really had become a loving family and were bound together in unity. We had never experienced anything quite like it before. We were experiencing the true hallmark of Christians. As Jesus said, 'By this all men will know that you are my disciples, if you have love for one another' (John 13:35).

Predictably this became an area of a major attack from the enemy. He didn't make a frontal attack by introducing little frictions, as he so often does. That would have been useless because, if we had anything against anyone, we met and talked, prayed, repented and fellowship was restored. No, the enemy tried a more subtle approach. Slowly and almost imperceptibly, two things began to happen. We began to 'protect' our unity in an inappropriate way. We began to try to agree on everything. If we didn't agree we kept quiet. Uniformity was being substituted for unity.

This led on to a more serious area. Some began to expect uniformity of spiritual experiences. A missionary friend who had arrived some time after the 'mini-revival', started talking about being 'baptised in the Spirit'. We had been talking about and experiencing the 'fullness of the Spirit' and had come to see the need for daily infilling.

'What exactly do you mean by the baptism of the Spirit?' Bill asked him one day, not just to discuss terminology, but with a genuine desire to know.

'Brother, if you'd had it, you would know,' was the unexpected reply. There was no room for discussion. There was no room for a slight difference of opinion on the meaning of a phrase which many great theologians, teachers and ordinary Christians have been disagreeing on for generations! We were soon divided into two camps. And there began to be a tendency to hark back to 'an experience', rather than to go on with the Lord.

A conference speaker who had been with us at the height of our unity and joy in the Lord, returned for a second visit.

'Some of you missionaries have fossilized your experience of a few years ago. Your love for the Lord was real and fresh and vibrant then. Now you are living in the past,' he protested, as he tried to encourage us to go on with the Lord. We were certainly in danger of dividing ourselves into groups by focusing on terminology rather than on our Lord.

Individuals in unity

The important lesson that we learnt was that God treats us as individuals. We are not identical and he will not give us identical experiences. Our conversion experiences are different. Our experiences of the Lord as we move on will be different. Our gracious heavenly Father will give us special experiences. Let's thank him for them. He will answer our prayers to reveal himself to us. Let's thank him and go on with him. Whatever the way in which God deals with us, whatever our theology of one-stage, two-stage or multiple-stage blessing, the important thing is that it is through love and true unity and not uniformity of experience, that the world is going to know that we are Jesus' disciples.

The biblical pattern is unity in diversity. Paul speaks of the church as the body of Christ. The body is made up of many parts – hands, feet, eyes, stomach – how different they all are. Compare a hand with an eye. The one, strong, shapely, flexible, capable of doing the most intricate things; the other, a more or less round wet object which looks rather unattractive if you see it in isolation. But it has the marvellous gift of sight. Hands and eyes are totally different. They are both useless without the head. In the body they need each other. Without one or the other, the body is severely handicapped.

'The eye cannot say to the hand, "I don't need you!"' says Paul in 1 Corinthians 12:21, and he also points out that 'If the foot should say, "Because I am not a hand, I do not belong to the body," it would not for that reason cease to be part of the body' (1 Corinthians 12:15).

The 'reformed' among us cannot say to the 'charismatics', 'I don't need you.' Nor can the 'charismatics' say to the 'reformed', 'I don't need you.' Nor can we say, 'Because you are not like me, you are not part of the body.' We need each other. Each has a contribution to the other and to the health of the body, provided each is living in submission to the Head. Whether we like it or not, we are all part of the body. We need to recognize and accept our differences and live together in loving unity, and not demand uniformity of one another. If the devil can drive a wedge between us on the basis of thinking that uniformity is unity, then the world will not see that the Father sent the Son, as Jesus prayed in his high priestly prayer: 'May they be brought to complete unity to let the world know that you sent me and have loved them even as you have loved me' (John 17:23).

Gifts – and the giver

There are not only different experiences. There are different gifts. Again, we need to live together in unity, not all expecting to have the same gifts. And it is the Holy Spirit who chooses which gifts he will give to each of us (1 Corinthians 12:11). We should not envy one another's gifts. Nor should we push our gifts onto others.

We experienced a most wonderful example of this harmony of different gifts when we returned to Sabah in 1984. We had not been in Borneo when God visited the church in the major revival of 1973 to 1974, though on subsequent visits we were able to share in some of the new and lively meetings which resulted. The revival continued to have ripples in various directions over the last twelve years and it seemed that the ripples had reached Meligan earlier in the year of our visit. Or was it the enemy imitating revival?

On arrival in Sabah we kept hearing rumours of strange things happening in Meligan.

'People are collapsing on the floor in the services' we were told. 'And they are going around pretending to be aeroplanes.'

Trances had been very much a feature of the 1974 revival. Frequently people had collapsed on the floor under the weight of conviction of sin. Some had even been unconscious for up to three hours, after which they would get up full of praise, rejoicing and thanking God for his forgiveness and blessing. Others had fallen into trances and God had spoken through them to bring conviction of sin to one and another.

'Go to X's farm hut. You will find a charm at the top of the right hand door post,' was the sort of message given. On that occasion it was the farm hut of one of the lay leaders of the church. He had hotly denied the existence of the charm. Nevertheless the other leaders had taken him to the farm hut. They had found the charm exactly where they had been told and the lay leader had fallen down under conviction of sin. He had come to a lasting repentance.

The collapsing on the floor, therefore, did not perturb us. If God chose to work that way (even though later on there was some counterfeiting), who were we to say anything against it? But pretending to be aeroplanes! That didn't sound very spiritual and we couldn't think what profit it could be at all. We really couldn't see how God could use such a strange phenomenon. But the rumours were persistent.

'Yes. Some of the women run round with their arms outstretched like aeroplanes. They have their eyes tight shut but they don't bump into anything.'

Stranger and stranger. Our thoughts went back to the cults we had heard about before the war. The Tagals were reputedly very unstable. Could the enemy have got in again? Our schedule was already far too tight, but we longed to visit them. We had been part of God's original 'scaffolding' in the building of that church. It appeared they also longed to see us.

We were at a mainly Lun Bawang convention not far from the borders of Tagal country. What joy to discover 150 Tagals from Meligan who had made the journey to the convention – a journey which used to be several days' walk but was now an expensive and very rough ride by jeep.

Bill had several hours talking with a group of them. Some were leaders. Some were ordinary church members with special gifts. One after another explained what happened to them when the Spirit 'came on them'.

Testing the spirits

'Is this from God?' they kept asking. 'You are our father. Please tell us. We don't want to do anything that is wrong.' After several hours, Bill was convinced that God was working but he was not sure whether it was all from God.

'If it's from God, we must not quench the Spirit. If the enemy is involved, we must pray against him,' he encouraged them, and suggested that they might lead us all in worship after the final session that night. They readily agreed.

'But we will want you to tell us at the end whether what we are doing is from God,' they added.

What a responsibility!

It was 11 p.m. when the final meeting closed. We had been sitting for three hours on hard, narrow benches. We were tired. The last thing we wanted was to stay on till midnight, but we had promised. Some of the Lun Bawang began to drift away. Then the Tagals started singing. Our reluctance disappeared. It was almost as if we were lifted up to heaven. It was not singing in tongues. (It was sometimes in Tagal, sometimes in Malay.) They were songs that had been given to them when they had been 'in the Spirit'. It was so wonderful, we were no longer tired. The Lun Bawang started to come back. We all shared with them in worship, confession of sin, testimony, exercise of various gifts, body ministry, preaching and exhortation. We were greatly enriched and refreshed, even though the meeting finally ended at 3 a.m.

We saw for ourselves the 'aeroplanes'! It was true what we had heard. They ran quite fast, eyes tight shut, jumping over benches but never slipping or bumping into anything. While this was going on, there were visions, tongues, interpretation of the tongues, enacted parables, and each one ended by collapsing on the floor. We felt transported back to Corinth and wanted to shout with Paul, 'one at a time' and 'do all things decently and in order'.

We were both praying for discernment for Bill, and for good fruit, ('By their fruit you will recognise them,' Matthew 7:16) so that he would know if it was from the Lord. And we prayed that the Lord would keep the enemy away. He answered all three requests. We witnessed repentance from sin, family reconciliation and sharing in ministry to a distraught woman. We were sure it was from God. The women who were cruising around were expelling the spirits from our midst and Bill was able to point out that it is the Lord alone who can do that. He warned them of the danger of 'taking on the devil' ourselves. Only the Lord himself is powerful enough for that. Not even an archangel will attempt it (Jude 9).

What was so wonderful, apart from the sense of God's presence, was the attitude to the distribution of gifts. Fourteen of the ordinary church members – young, old, male, female – had received special gifts. The leaders had not received any new and spectacular gifts. Frequently the preaching was by one of the leaders who had been given a passage on which to preach by someone who had received a word from the Lord. There seemed to be no rivalry. Those who had received these special gifts in no way looked down on those without, nor were they pushing for others to seek the gifts. Those without were in no way jealous of those with new gifts. They were working in harmony 'so that the body of Christ may be built up' (Ephesians 4:12). On one occasion at Meligan, when the pastor was told what to preach and he preached on the given passage, eighty people came under deep conviction of sin. Lives were being changed.

'I don't really understand what is happening,' the native chief said. 'But whatever it is, I am happy. My people are living together in much greater harmony.'

Of thumb-nails and rams

We returned from the convention to Kota Kinabalu where the SIB in Sabah has its headquarters. We shared with Arun, the Chairman, what we felt about Meligan. He too had heard the strange rumours, and had been to Meligan just a few weeks before we had arrived. He had had a rather unnerving but blessed experience.

He shared with them in worship, as we had done. After a time a man came up to him.

'Show me your thumb-nails,' he said.

Arun hesitatingly held out his hands.

'Are you willing to give your thumb-nails as a token of your love for the Lord?' the Tagal man asked him.

Arun felt the blood drain from his face. His heart pounded. There was perhaps some truth in the rumours that the Tagals had gone a bit crazy. Arun is a Lun Bawang and no doubt he was tempted to fear these unpredictable Tagals. What was he to do? With an SOS prayer for wisdom, he replied, 'Yes, if that is what the Lord wants. But I do not know that that is what he wants.'

'Let us ask the Lord,' the man replied, and the whole church erupted in simultaneous and enthusiastic prayer. As it died down, the man asked the same question and Arun gave the same reply.

'Come outside,' the man requested and Arun followed, not knowing what was going to happen, but with a sense of peace that God was in control.

'Look in the grass,' the man suggested.

Arun bent down and began to feel in the grass. He felt something hard. He picked it up. It was a ten cent piece. He held it up.

'Oh, wonderful!' his Tagal friend exclaimed. 'Isn't that good of the Lord. He has given you a ten cent piece to offer to him instead of your thumb-nails.' He paused. 'Now God wants you to preach on Abraham offering up Isaac!'

The congregation was hushed as they walked back into the church, and they listened intently as Arun preached on the wonderful provision of the ram and the even more wonderful provision of the Lord Jesus Christ as Saviour.

Arun explained to us that he had preached with much more feeling and understanding than he had ever done before. And the Lord had spoken to his hearers. We were not surprised!

The exercise of the gifts with the exposition of the Word – charismata with teaching. It was a lovely combination, and was being used by the Lord to bring conviction of sin and a growing maturity to these Tagal folk. We came home praising the Lord for his intervention and with our own hearts 'strangely warmed'.

When we pray for revival, do we know what we are asking for? Or are we praying with unconscious conditions? Are we prepared for God to do unusual things on the one hand or on the other hand are we *insisting* that he performs signs and wonders? Some who pray for revival give the impression that they would want to stop it if God were to do unusual things. Others seem to think it could not be revival unless God did unusual things. 'The wind blows wherever it pleases' (John 3:8). We cannot dictate to God. He will work in his way and that will be the most suitable and effective for the particular time, place, culture and language.

To think about

Meditate on the unity and extraordinary diversity of the body as an illustration of the body of Christ, i.e. the church. See 1 Corinthians 12:12–31.

Bookshelf

You are my God, David Watson (Hodder and Stoughton, 1983).
A very readable and worthwhile book with particularly helpful chapters on 'Baptism or Fulness' and 'Tensions and Divisions'.

Joy Unspeakable, D. Martin Lloyd-Jones (Kingsway Publications, 1984).
This is a book which should be read by all who are hungry for a deeper experience of God (hopefully that is all of us!). It is sub-titled 'The Baptism with the Holy Spirit' and it is important that we do not allow any disagreement over terminology to keep us from seeking the reality of a deeper experience of

the working of the Holy Spirit in our lives.

The Message of 1 Corinthians: Life in the local church, David Prior (IVP, The Bible Speaks Today series, 1985; UK and US editions).
A most helpful commentary. David Prior deals with chapters 12 to 14 with great insight and sensitivity.

The Message of Ephesians: God's New Society, John R. W. Stott (IVP, The Bible Speaks Today series, 1979; UK and US editions).
A very stimulating commentary. Relevant to our subject in this chapter, John Stott's comments on Unity and Diversity in chapter 7, and the filling of the Spirit in chapter 9 are particularly helpful.

Keep in Step With the Spirit, J. I. Packer (IVP, 1984; first published in the USA by Fleming H. Revell Company).
The author gives us a comprehensive study of the work of the Holy Spirit in the Bible, in the history of the church and at present, with a timely reminder that 'there is nothing so Spirit-quenching as to study the Spirit's work without being willing to be touched, humbled, convicted and changed as you go along.' Having looked at an interpretation of the charismatic life in chapter 6, Jim Packer ends with a plea in his final chapter that we should not be satisfied with where we are, but that we should be praying for revival.

9

The powers of darkness

*Corrie • The return of fear • An example of two
soldiers • Involvement • Freedom at last • The devil is
real • 'An angel of light' • A subtle enemy*

Fear, like a thick wet blanket, was smothering me. It
was no ordinary fear. True, I was able to push it aside
while I got on with the job of translating or talking to
people or caring for the children, but as soon as I
stopped doing something, there it was. It was taking
over my life. I fought it for days. Bill and I prayed.
But still it kept coming back.

The big problem was – we couldn't find any logic
to it. For some reason or other, a crisis in the Middle
East had triggered it off and whenever Bill turned
on our radio to listen to the news, I went out of the
room. I wanted to be an ostrich and bury my head in
the sand. But why so consumed with dread about
something which was happening so far away?

One night I stood on the verandah of our little
bamboo and bark house at Meligan. I looked out at
the beautiful mountains surrounding the village. All
was peace and quiet but for the familiar buzzing of
the jungle night life. I thought of those lovely words:

'As the mountains surround Jerusalem,
so the LORD surrounds his people
both now and for evermore.' (Psalm 125:2)

My heart was warmed and I felt at peace – but only for a moment. As I continued to look, the sky seemed blacker than I had ever seen it and a cold shudder went through me. What was happening in that blackness beyond the mountains? The fear gripped me again, and my mind started racing round in circles. The events in the Middle East might trigger off a world war. We would never be able to get home. War would spread and we would be interned. Internment. That was it. I could never cope with that.

I had heard a lot about Japanese internment camps from our friends who had been in Borneo before the war. Frank Davidson had died mainly due to the privations of internment. I had heard their stories of the ruthless discipline of the Japanese, but of course had not experienced the special and daily grace which God had given them in their time of need. We don't get strength for tomorrow's needs or for someone else's problems. I had forgotten how this was so clearly illustrated in the wonderful experience that Winsome Southwell had had as she and her husband had paddled downriver to give themselves up in order to save the tribal people from reprisals. 'What are the Japanese *to me*,' God had said to her, and flooded her heart with a peace which never left her in all the three years of internment.

Bill had reminded me many a time that 'My grace is sufficient for you [singular], for my power is made perfect in weakness' (2 Corinthians 12:9), and 'As your days, so shall your strength be' (Deuteronomy 33:25, RSV). He had reminded me that most of our friends had survived internment. He reminded me too of God's sovereignty, in which I so firmly believed. It was all very logical, and normally would have restored my confidence in God. Bill usually has just the right thing to say to bring me back onto an even keel. But not in this situation. He had no answer, either as a doctor or as a Christian. Prayer didn't seem to make much difference either. However much we prayed, the overwhelming fear returned, often when I was least expecting it.

Corrie

The Middle East crisis ended. The fear subsided, returning only intermittently over the next couple of years, and never with the same force. I learnt to avoid listening to the news or reading certain books. But then a situation arose when I needed to read *A prisoner – and yet*, by Corrie ten Boom. She was travelling through south-east Asia and was coming to visit us in Borneo. As Bill was acting Field Chairman at the time, we expected to be giving her hospitality. It seemed appropriate to read her book. Several of the other missionaries had read it and said it was a marvellous story but they had said enough to alert Bill. I read it but, thanks to his warning, I skipped the chapter on her sister Betsie's death in the prison camp.

Corrie lived with us for a couple of weeks of fun, laughter and serious discussion. She had an endless fund of stories, many of them dramatic, frequently amusing (the way she told them, anyway), but always glorifying to her 'heavenly father'. We were greatly blessed by this old (as she called herself) lady's marvellous trust and faith in God. Again and again I marvelled at her serenity and her great 'humanness'. Because of her positive trust, I could listen to her stories about internment without fear. God was in control.

The story that made the biggest impression on me concerned the SS guard who had beaten her sister while she was dying. Corrie was taking a meeting in Germany. As the people filed out, she saw a man coming down the aisle to meet her. He was well-dressed and smiling. But all she could see was a man in SS uniform. He was the man they had most feared and hated.

'Miss ten Boom, I am now your brother in Christ,' he said as he put out his hand to greet her.

'My arm was like lead at my side,' Corrie told us, 'and in the few seconds of hesitation I argued with God. "Why Lord?" I asked. "Why should you save that man? He deserved hell. Why should you have mercy on him? Why should you save him when he helped to kill my sister?" And I just wanted to run away.'

But God had insisted, 'You love him for my sake.'

'Oh, no, Lord, you can't ask me to do that,' she had protested.

'You love him for my sake and Betsie's. He's now my child.'

'It's not fair, you can't ask me to do that, Lord.'

And then she thought of what she had just been preaching – love and forgiveness. 'Well, you'll have to help me, Lord,' she prayed, somewhat reluctantly.

She had then gone on to explain to us the miracle that happened as she truly forgave that cruel guard. God's power seemed to come into her arm and lift it up to shake hands with her former captor. 'I experienced God's love filling my heart for that man,' she added. 'It was a miracle. It could not have happened any other way.' And we could see that she meant it.

Why should I fear internment or even the death of a loved one, if God could bring such blessing from it? Corrie was such fun. She had no emotional scars. Her faith and trust in God were so real and she had been a blessing to thousands.

Corrie travelled extensively through post-war Europe and found a lot of real spiritual darkness. She was constantly meeting those who had become involved in some way or other with the occult. We were so impressed with what she was telling us that we arranged for her to spend a week in a Rest House up in the hills at the Mission's expense, so that she could write it all up. *Defeated Enemies* was the result – a book which has helped hundreds who have inadvertently or deliberately got involved with the occult. But still it did not occur to us that I might be in that position myself.

The return of fear

Several years later, my illogical, oppressive fears returned. This time it was confrontation between Indonesia and Malaysia which triggered things off. Again it was so illogical, as I had gone through facing death during the Brunei Rebellion with extraordinary calm some months before.

Bill and I began to think about what Corrie had been telling us about spirit oppression, which she clearly differentiated from spirit possession. 'Could it be?' we queried.

Just to ask the question seemed to answer it.

'But what do we do about it?' We had had little teaching in our home churches on the subject.

We remembered Corrie speaking about spirit oppression in post-war Europe. Many had been uncertain about soldiers who were 'missing'. Were they still in Russian concentration camps, or had they died during the fighting? The uncertainty had caused many relatives to go to fortune-tellers and Corrie had found that again and again, this had resulted in a great spiritual darkness. She had also explained to us that, whenever she spoke against the sin of involvement with the occult, she too had become oppressed. She often became so tired that she could hardly reach her bed. Her heart began to beat irregularly and she felt ill. She tells of one incident in *Defeated Enemies*.

'One evening I had a long talk with my heavenly Father. "I cannot continue like this, dear Lord. Why must I give this message? Why must I testify against this particular sin? So many of your faithful servants never mention it! I can't go on like this much longer, and live! Perhaps another month or two, and then my heart will give out!"

'Then in the *Losungsbuch* [a daily devotional book in German] I read, "Be not afraid, but speak, and hold not thy peace. For I am with thee and no man shall set on thee to hurt thee" (Acts 18:9–10). A short poem follows,

> "Though all the powers of hell attack
> Fear not, Jesus is Victor."

'Joy filled my heart. This was God's answer. I prayed, "Lord, I will obey, I will not fear and be silent. But with my hands on this promise, I ask You to protect me with Your blood, that the demons cannot touch me."

'At that moment something happened to my heart; it beat regularly. I knew that I was healed. After this, having spoken against sorcery and witchcraft, I felt as well as ever before; Jesus is Victor. The fear of demons comes from demons themselves. We have nothing to fear. He who is with us is greater than those who are against us! Hidden with Christ in God; what a refuge! The mighty High Priest, and His legions of angels, are on our side.'

But I had not been to fortune-tellers. We had certainly been working in enemy territory and seeing the Word 'mighty through God to the pulling down of strongholds'. But I had not consciously done anything which might have given the enemy a foothold in my life.

An example of two soldiers

Then we discussed Corrie's example of soldiers on reconnaissance – an example we have used and enlarged upon many a time since, when we have been asked to speak on the occult.

Imagine two soldiers on reconnaissance. They drop their compass. Wisely they don't light a match to try to look for it. They fumble around in the deep mud. No good. The compass is lost. It's a dark night, so there are no stars. They will have to try to get back to their lines. They wander around, lost. Eventually they think they have made it, only to find to their dismay that they have strayed into enemy territory. Naturally they are captured.

Corrie used to explain.

'It's no good the soldiers saying, "Oh, excuse me, please, it was not my intention to come here. I just came by mistake." '

Whether intentionally or unintentionally, once you are in their terrain, you are at risk of capture.

How do we open the door to enemy oppression in this way? Corrie lists a number of things: 'witch-craft, sorcery, magic (black and white) or fortune-telling, wearing of charms or amulets, or contact with false doctrines or with persons who exercise demonic influence such as witch-doctors and medicine men and fortune-tellers or "wise women" or spiritualists...or people who foretell the future from cards or from the lines of one's hand.' And we could add ouija boards, levitation, glass-moving, seances, and the like.

Involvement

Not all involvement in these things leads to spirit oppression but some does, and it is therefore impor-tant that we steer clear of all of it. The evidence in my case was clear. I had certainly been involved and when I became a Christian as a student, I remember describing it to my pastor.

'It's as if my feet were just on the edge of a huge precipice. God snatched me back right from the very edge.' But that was some twelve years before that horrible experience at Meligan. I had repented. Surely it couldn't really be connected?

Though I had rejoiced in God's saving grace, and repented of my sin and my immediate involvement with the occult, I hadn't really thought of earlier situations. It seemed that I needed to repent specifi-cally of those too. The enemy may wait years before he takes up his options. It is important, as Corrie says 'to go back and close the door exactly where you opened it...confess your sin, ask forgiveness and give thanks for it... Then the door is closed, and you are free. Then you are no longer at the demon's mercy.'

'Lord, we are children,' we prayed. 'We don't know how to go out or come in. We are quite inexperienced and helpless. But you have said, "Resist the devil and he will flee from you." Therefore in the name and on the authority of the Lord Jesus Christ we resist him and tell him to flee and to go back to the abyss where he belongs. Protect us and the children by the precious blood of Christ.'

Freedom at last

A very simple prayer. Some, who have been brought up during a period of much greater awareness of enemy activity, may call it naive. But Jesus the Victor gave us the authority to pray it. Nothing dramatic happened, but I felt free and relieved.

A few weeks later Bill set off for a six-month speaking tour of Australia, New Zealand and New Guinea. I went back to Tagal country. I felt very alone (eighteen miles' walk from the nearest Government post and telephone to the outside world). I was a good target for the enemy. I arrived in the village to be told that Indonesian guerillas had been seen not far away in the jungle. Immediately that wet blanket began to come down. But immediately also I claimed the victory of Christ, and the protection of his blood shed on the cross.

'In Jesus' name you are to leave me alone,' I almost shouted. 'And leave Bill and the children alone too.

Protect us all, Lord, by the blood and victory of your cross.' The blanket lifted, leaving me feeling as if I had a wall of protection around me. I had peace and that peace remained all through my time there. I was able to get on with the job of translating and ministering to the church. To this day, I have never had another attack like it. But whenever we speak of the occult, we always pray for that wall of protection for us and the family.

The devil is real

Since that time, there has been a much greater awareness of the reality of the devil and the activity of evil spirits in the West. In 1971, Bill spoke on the subject at a young people's camp, where ages ranged from twelve to eighteen. He asked how many of the youngsters had ever been involved, or had friends who had been involved, with ouija boards, glass-moving, levitation, and the like. Uninhibited, all but one put up their hands – including the twelve-year-old daughter of one of the officers. He was dumbfounded!

A little later, after frequently being asked to speak on the occult both in the East *and* in the West, Bill commented:

'The older generation of faculty members, Christian or not, tend to laugh at the idea of evil spirits. They may accept that "primitive" people have strange experiences but not the more "civilized" people of Western society. But with the younger generation, the students, it is a totally different situation. They know only too well that the forces of evil are real and very present.' After one Christian

Union meeting a girl came up to him.

'You don't need to convince us of the reality of evil spirits. We know all too well they exist.' And she went on to explain that she had been one of four girls who had run a seance together during their first year at university.

'And how were you saved from it?' Bill queried.

'I was living on the same corridor as Ali' (pointing to one of the CU members). 'She started praying for me and telling me about Jesus. I have become a Christian.'

'And what about the others?'

'It's awful,' she said. 'One is in a mental hospital. One has dropped out of the course, and I've lost touch with her. One has become a hippie.'

It was now her turn to pray for her three friends.

'An angel of light'

While the enemy has been showing himself more overtly in the West, the reverse has been frequently happening in Borneo. The 'roaring lion' has become an 'angel of light'.

Bill was visiting villages all over Tagal country. He and some Tagal Christians were slipping and slithering their way along the river when they came to a stretch where it passed a huge rock. They clambered on to the bank where a path, trodden out by hundreds of feet over the years, made a huge detour around this rock, which was the 'home' of many evil spirits. For centuries, no Tagal had dared to go near it.

Bill was not quite sure what was happening when one young man, Ibin, took out his jungle knife and slashed his way off the path towards the rock. The others joined him. In an instinctive act of joy and triumph, Ibin ran ahead and jumped up on to the top of the rock. He stamped his foot.

'Who fears Satan now?' he shouted and stamped again and again as the others, still a little fearful to get too close, joined in the shouting. Ibin and his friends were Christians now. They had proved so many times that Jesus is stronger than Satan. Ibin was exuberant.

Bill called him down. 'Let's get out our Bibles,' and there in the jungle, at the foot of 'Satan's rock', and after prayer for protection, he led them in studying what God had to say. Yes, certainly Jesus is Victor and wants us to enjoy his freedom and his triumph. Certainly he has routed the enemy and we do not need to fear him. But Bill foresaw a danger in Ibin's attitude. Was the devil doing a 'disappearing trick', as he had done for so long in the West while still having control of so many lives?

'Look at Jude, verse 9,' Bill suggested.

Ibin began to read: 'But even the archangel Michael, when he was disputing with the devil about the body of Moses, did not dare to bring a slanderous accusation against him, but said, "The Lord rebuke you!"'

'How powerful is an archangel?' Bill asked, using his usual method of asking questions. In this way the Tagals themselves found what God was saying rather than Bill just telling them. They thought about it.

'We don't know,' they finally decided, after some discussion. Bill suggested that they read about the angel who went through the whole of Egypt in one night killing all the firstborn.

134

'Was that angel powerful?' he asked.

'Phew, very,' they replied.

'And Jude is talking about an archangel – that's a leader of angels,' Bill went on.

'An archangel must be very, very powerful,' one of the Tagals suggested.

'Yes, indeed. But did the archangel Michael tackle the devil in his own strength?' Bill continued to question.

'No. He said, "The Lord rebuke you!" ' they replied.

'Should we then try to take on the enemy in our own strength?'

'No, we must trust in God's strength.'

There, sitting beneath the rock which they no longer needed to fear, they prayed for forgiveness, for further enlightenment, and for the protection of the blood of Christ. And they praised God for the freedom into which they had entered through faith in him. Then they continued on their way to tell other Tagals of the wonderful victory of Christ and of his love for them. As they walked along, Bill pondered that we had failed to teach adequately the doctrine of the devil, because we had somehow unconsciously felt that they knew more about him than we did. Certainly they knew him as a roaring lion, but they had yet to learn how to cope with him as an angel of light.

A subtle enemy

The first turning of these Tagals from darkness to light had been very consciously from total submission to the power of the devil to submission to the loving power of God. Only secondly did they come to Jesus for forgiveness. In the West we have tended to preach the forgiveness of sins and not to realize the reality of the devil. He is very subtle. As we, in the West, become aware of him, he will make us fear him and come under direct bondage. As the Tagals, who were already aware of him, came to see that Jesus could give them victory over him, he started operating as an angel of light.

'This stone is a good stone. It only helps me to do good things and to help people. I don't need to destroy that with all the other bad things, do I?' was a question we were often asked.

We had to teach that Jesus alone is sufficient. White magic or black, good or bad charms, they all have the same origin. But many did not even ask the question. They just hid one or two charms. Just as in the materialistic West, we do not turn from all our materialistic attitudes when we become Christians, so in Borneo, they did not throw out all their charms and fetishes. They just kept one or two that were not really 'evil', just in case they might need them later on.

When revival came to the interior of Sabah and Sarawak in 1973 and 1974, God convicted many a man and woman of harbouring a few 'charms'.

'This stone is like my telephone to God. I talk to it and I hear God talking to me through it. It can't be bad, can it?' was the difficult question put to us by a pastor. Dare we suggest he should throw out his aid to prayer?

'Now that I have thrown out my charms, the people don't fear me and respect me as much as they used to,' a native chief complained to us. 'What can I do about it?'

In the village of Bario, the headmaster had a charm which he felt helped him in discussion and debate with those who might be opposed to him. He had just become a Christian in the first week or so of the revival, but he had hung on to this charm. He'd thrown away all the others. But God couldn't want him to throw this one away. He had an important meeting in a few days' time. He might need it.

On the night of the meeting, he decided to call in on the young people's prayer meeting to make sure all was well. He had to go past the school. He would only stay for a few minutes. Hardly had he stepped inside at the back of the hall, when he heard one of the student leaders speaking.

'There is someone here holding something evil in his hand. It is very powerful.'

The headmaster tightened his grip on the charm in his pocket. They could not know about it – it was very small. They must be referring to something else. Someone else spoke up.

'There is someone important in this room and he is holding something evil.' And then, a few minutes later, 'He is a very important person in our school.'

The headmaster never reached his meeting that night. He stood before his own students and staff and confessed his reluctance to part with this most powerful of his charms.

We do not need to fear the devil because Jesus is Victor. But we need to recognize his existence and his activity, whether it is overt or subtle. Only then will we be able to resist him in Jesus' name. Then he will have to flee from us. Jesus defeated the principalities and powers on the cross making 'a show of them openly' (Colossians 2:15, AV), and so we stand victorious with him. He is Victor.

To think about

1. Are we aware enough of Matthew 12:29 and 2 Corinthians 4:4? How should this affect our praying for the conversion/deliverance of friends in the United Kingdom and overseas?

2. Not all temptation and testing come directly from the Evil One. Compare Matthew 15:19–20, James 1:14 and James 4:1–3 with Luke 4:1–2, 13, 1 Timothy 4:1 and 1 Thessalonians 3:5.

Bookshelf

The Fight, John White (IVP, 1977; first published in the USA).
Look especially at chapter 5, 'His Infernal Majesty', which deals with the reality of the devil, with response to temptation, and with the devil as an 'accuser of the brethren'. John White goes on to show how the deceiver can be overcome, and discusses the armour available to us in our warfare with Satan.

The Masks of Melancholy, John White (UK and US editions, IVP, 1982).
In his discussion on demons and mental illness, John White wisely points out that there are two extremes to be avoided. 'Enthusiasts who seem over-eager both to spot demons and to bind them, exorcise them or consign them to outer darkness where they belong...at the other extreme are Christians who do not believe in demons at all...yet the middle of the road also has its dangers...'

The Screwtape Letters, C. S. Lewis (Fontana, 1955).
In his preface to this brilliant little book, C.S. Lewis makes a similar statement: 'There are two equal and opposite errors into which our race can fall about the devils. One is to disbelieve in their existence. The other is to believe, and to feel an excessive and unhealthy interest in them. They themselves are equally pleased by both errors and hail a materialist or a magician with the same delight.' The book consists of a series of letters from a senior devil to a junior devil, advising him how best to handle the 'patient' who has been allocated to him.

Defeated Enemies, Corrie ten Boom (Christian Literature Crusade, 1968).
A small but invaluable book which has helped thousands to see that they can be delivered from oppression from the evil one.

Born for Battle, R. Arthur Mathews (OMF, 1979; now jointly published with STL).
Most of the thirty-one studies on spiritual warfare first appeared as editorials in the OMF magazine, *East Asia Millions*. 'In his Gethsemane struggle', Mathews writes, 'the Lord Jesus teaches us two important things: submit to God and resist the devil. God's warfare against Satan is carried on by his submissive people actively resisting Satan by insisting at all costs "Thy will be done on earth as it is in heaven".'

I believe in Satan's downfall, Michael Green (Hodder and Stoughton, 1981).
Michael Green looks at the biblical account of evil and the possibility of its defeat. It is a very relevant,

up-to-date book, bringing an awareness of Satan's power and influence in our world today without leaving us defeated or depressed. The book ends with a look at the destruction of Satan, and the possibility of Christians overcoming 'by the blood of the Lamb and by the word of their testimony, for they loved not their lives unto death'.

The Message of Revelation: I Saw Heaven Opened, Michael Wilcock (IVP, The Bible Speaks Today series, 1975; US and UK editions).
A most useful and balanced exposition of a difficult book. It is easy to read and will encourage us in time of difficulty, giving us a renewed awareness of the sovereignty of our God and his ultimate destruction of Satan.

10

Disciple-making and disappointments

A church in decline ● *What had gone wrong?* ● *Some answers* ● *The parable of the sower* ● *Jesus and Peter* ● *Applying the lesson to Borneo* ● *The example of Paul* ● *Real wounds* ● *Purait*

'Have we achieved anything?'

'Were we wrong to encourage new Christians to share their faith when they knew so little themselves?'

'Were we wrong to insist that the church supported its own pastor?'

'Were our missionary methods all wrong?'

'Should we have stayed and not moved on?'

We were taking stock. Though we had experienced God working in our lives, and in the church at Meligan, ten years after our first visit the situation looked a bit grim. We had moved from this thriving church to another area where the language was more appropriate for the translation of the New Testament. The Meligan church was already governing itself, supporting its own pastor and active in evangelism. In fact all the churches in the area to which we had moved had been planted by Meligan Tagals. One had been established by ten families who had moved to live there, several others by folk who had passed through for trade or spent a few months in casual labour on the rubber plantations. We had been so excited to see the establishment of 'daughter' and even 'granddaughter' churches to the Meligan church – about twenty in all. Even apart from the need to change dialects, it had seemed appropriate to move on to give the church freedom. They needed scope to do things their way under the direction of the Holy Spirit and not to be constantly looking to us for advice.

A church in decline

Five years after moving we were wondering whether we had been unwise. The church at Meligan was in a pathetic state. Amat, too, had moved on to pioneer two more successive areas, but his wife was more and more longing for the companionship of her own Lun Bawang people, and the comfort of using her own language.

They had pulled out of the ministry, not because they believed that God had called them to return home, but because they had had enough. Who could blame them? They were already quite old when they had gone into Bible School to learn to read and study for the first time. They were even older when they had gone to their former head-hunting enemies to pioneer evangelism, and to establish a church. They had learnt to speak Tagal fluently, albeit with a strong Lun Bawang accent, and often with some Lun Bawang sentence structures. They had learnt to live alongside the Tagals, trudge up and down their mountains and eat their food. The Tagals loved them. Their own Lun Bawang people, however, were very much more prosperous since they had become Christians some years before, and given up their chronic alcoholism. Amat and his wife longed for a few home comforts. They longed too for the security of their own extended family, where they could be cared for and supported as they grew older, and not to be the main burden-bearers.

Amat's place as pastor had been taken by the headman's younger brother. He had been one of the first two Tagals ever to go into Bible School. This in itself was a courageous act as the school was two days' walk away over the mountains, and situated in the middle of Lun Bawang country. During their vacations, they had eagerly instructed their own people in the ways of this new Christian faith which they had adopted. They had been a little unreliable in school, but they seemed to follow all that they understood, and had been allowed to graduate. The headman had insisted that they would not support any pastor other than his brother. We were a little concerned about this, as we suspected the reason was that it would be easier and cheaper to support his brother, who would automatically help with the family farm. We wondered how much time he would get for his pastoral work. Nevertheless we were not in a position to impose anyone on them. It was their choice.

This young man did not last many years as pastor (in spite of the devotion and commitment of his wife), and his place was taken by a Lun Bawang (rather less forceful than Amat), and then by a Tagal lay leader acting as pastor. The congregation steadily dwindled during this period until finally the people decided that they could not afford to have a pastor at all.

Side by side with these changes, there had been political upheavals. The Tagal ex-pastor had gone into politics, and soon accepted the advantages of becoming a Muslim. The Brunei Rebellion and confrontation with Indonesia which followed shortly afterwards, meant that this border area became an army outpost. The short and narrow airstrip was soon replaced by a longer and wider one which could take twin-engined aircraft. This meant that heavy loads of material goods could be brought in. The well-disciplined Gurkha soldiers were popular and did not interfere in the villages, but they were soon replaced by Malaysian soldiers. So-called Western 'civilization' invaded the area. The number attending the little church dropped to a mere handful.

What had gone wrong?

What was there of lasting value from our hard work, sacrifice of home and comfort, our prayers and the faithful praying of friends at home? Had our excitement in the Lord's apparent sovereign intervention been misplaced? Had we been wrong to hand over responsibility so soon to the local Tagal Christians? They were certainly keen on evangelism but should we have stayed longer, let the translation of the New Testament wait a while, and see that this one parent church was really well taught? Or should we perhaps have helped them a little financially so that they could have kept a pastor to continue to teach them? We came to the conclusion that our 'missionary methods' were basically right. What then had gone wrong?

Even on the medical side, which was a real success story, there were question marks. The health revolution had reversed the steady decline of the Tagals, not only at Meligan but in all the surrounding area. This however was also presenting problems. They seemed at times to be more interested in the health benefits of becoming Christians than in the power of Christ that had made the diet changes and health revolution possible. We had a number of 'rice' Christians – those who turned to Christianity purely for the material benefits.

It was not all negative however. There were daughter and granddaughter churches which seemed to be thriving, even if the parent church was not. And there were real flickers of hope at Meligan itself. One man whose conversion had been a very specific answer to very special prayer, was still standing firm, as was his family. The ex-pastor's wife had not followed him into Islam and was holding the Christian banner as high as she dare. Her brother and his wife, rather more shakily, were standing with her. There were one or two other families. But what was that out of more than 150, many of whom had regularly walked for hours to come to church on Sundays?

The Tagal translation was going well, and the church in the village where we were living was lively and enthusiastic – so were the little group of Meligan Tagals living an hour down the track from us. We were handing over responsibility as quickly as possible, they were supporting their own pastors, and were eagerly moving out in evangelism. Would the same thing, however, happen to them when we moved on? Was their main enthusiasm because they had medical help and the prestige of Western missionaries living in their midst?

Some answers

About this time, the Lord graciously drew Bill's attention to two things: firstly, two parables – the sower, and the weeds; secondly, the Lord's own ministry on earth, as well as that of Paul.

A comparison of the two parables, and a little bit of mathematics, shows that the 'field' can be divided into five areas. The first major division is in the good seed and the weeds – true believers and counterfeit Christians. The farmer sowed the seed and it was good seed. Immediately 'that night' – secretly – the enemy came and sowed the weeds. For quite a long time the weeds were practically indistinguishable from the wheat.

This obviously had happened at Meligan. In their early turning to Christ, there were those who truly put their faith in him. They were overwhelmed with the joy of deliverance from the fear of the evil spirits. They had discovered that Jesus is even stronger than Satan! They were born again. The control and authority of Satan had been exposed as no longer absolute. He reacted immediately, switching from an operation as the terrorizing 'roaring lion' to his deceiving 'angel of light' line of attack. We can see now that he was happy to 'liberate' his people from the crippling fear of spirit appeasement (animism) and the debilitating effects of chronic alcoholism and habitual adultery. He was even ready for them to attend services regularly – be good, counterfeit, nominal Christians – if that was the best way to keep them from personal faith in Jesus Christ. He had been exposed as a murderer and a destroyer. His purpose had not changed, but the tactics were totally different. He was prepared to give some ground in the short-term, with a view to maintaining his grip in the years ahead.

All this we could begin to understand as we studied the parable of the weeds. But nevertheless, the proportion seemed inordinately high. Was this our fault and had we, albeit in partnership with the Lord, got in his way so much that we had made a pretty bad job of sowing? Probably, but there were other factors.

The parable of the sower

The parable of the sower helped us here. Not all the good seed matured to the point of bearing fruit. Some seed fell by the wayside and 'the birds came and ate it up'. Some of the seed fell on rocky ground and some among the thorns. All this was either lost, failed to thrive, or was choked. Some, only some, fell on good ground, 'where it produced a crop – a hundred, sixty or thirty times what was sown' (Matthew 13).

Clearly these parables prepare us to face disappointments. There will be weeds as well as seed which falls by the wayside. We must be thankful when the difference between counterfeit Christians and true believers begins to show. We grieve over Christians who fail to thrive either through succumbing to the 'cares of this world' or giving way to opposition, but they are not counterfeit. It is the good seed of the word of God which has been sown in their hearts. We can therefore pray and believe that 'no-one can snatch them out of my Father's hand' (John 10:29).

What about the seed which falls on good ground?

147

They are the really committed Christians who mature, and bring fruit. We don't have to face disappointment there too, do we? We were learning that the answer is an emphatic 'yes'. God reminded us of what happened to the Lord over Peter, and later to Paul.

Jesus and Peter

Peter must have been 'good ground' – after all he was responsible under the anointing of the Holy Spirit for three thousand believers on the day of Pentecost. Nevertheless he had somewhat of an unreliable record as a disciple, which would surely have tempted us contemporary Christian workers to give up on him. He would have brought us near to despair. How did Jesus cope with him?

Right from the beginning, Jesus accepted the fact that his Father had chosen Peter. Had he not spent all night in prayer before the choice was made? We know that his communion with the Father was perfect, and he didn't do anything 'by himself' (John 5:19). He must therefore have been convinced that these twelve men were the ones his Father had chosen. Perhaps during that night of prayer, the Father was reassuring him that these were indeed his choice, even if they were not at first sight very promising material. Jesus could trust the Father – even to enable him to handle a disciple like Peter, who was going to bring him frequent disappointments as well as great encouragements.

Jesus taught Peter, shared his work with him and gave him some very special experiences and revelations. It was Peter to whom God gave the insight to say 'You are the Christ, the Son of the living God' (Matthew 16:16–17). It was a special revelation from the Father to him personally, yet in the very next paragraph he reveals a total ignorance of what that Sonship meant. He seeks to turn the Lord aside from obedience to his Father's will by tempting him to avoid the cross.

'Never, Lord! This shall never happen to you!' he blurts out (Matthew 16:22), or as another version expresses it, 'Pity yourself, Lord.'

He had experienced the endless self-giving of the Lord, and had listened to him explaining to them the need for the Son of Man to suffer and he says in effect:

'Think about yourself, Lord. Put yourself first. Don't let yourself be pushed into such suffering. Look after yourself.'

Had he learnt anything about the Son of God and his commitment?

Jesus recognized this as an attack from Satan and rebuked Peter with strong words:

'Out of my sight, Satan! You are a stumbling block to me; you do not have in mind the things of God, but the things of men' (Matthew 16:23).

What a heartbreak it must have been to the all-loving Son of God to have to speak like that to Peter, and how disappointed he must have been, especially after the special revelation Peter had just received.

Jesus did not give up on Peter. He graciously took him up the mountain with James and John, and there Peter was allowed to witness the transfiguration (Matthew 17). Imagine, however, the grief to Jesus when Peter, overwhelmed with excitement, gives the impression that he thinks of Moses, Elijah and Jesus as all in the same category.

'Lord, it is good for us to be here. If you wish, I will put up three shelters – one for you, one for Moses and one for Elijah.'

The Father intervenes and proclaims again, 'This is my Son.'

Not long after this, and maybe as a direct result of the special experience for Peter, James and John on the mountain, the disciples are reported as arguing as to who is the greatest (Luke 9:46). It's a temptation that comes to all of us when we have new and exciting experiences of the Lord, and we need to listen to the Lord's rebuke.

'He who is least among you all – he is the greatest' (Luke 9:48).

It was a very gentle rebuke, but none the less Jesus must have been very disappointed to have to give it.

Jesus knew Peter was chosen by the Father. He loved him. And there was another factor which kept him from 'writing off' Peter as one of the ones to whom he was going to hand over the evangelization of the world. True, he couldn't trust Peter not to make a mess of it. But he could trust the Holy Spirit whom he was going to send to him (John 16:7). He would guide him into all truth (John 16:13). He would remind him of what Jesus had taught him (John 14:26). He would give him power to be a witness (Acts 1:8 and 4:31).

Applying the lesson to Borneo

We knew there were born-again believers in Meligan. However much they had quenched the Spirit we could trust him to keep them, renew them and to 'fan into life' the flame that had first illuminated them. He would remind them of the teaching and lead them out once again to reach out to others.

We could even be encouraged to believe that he would use those who were just a 'smouldering wick' (which produces a smell rather than light). The Lord had said he would not snuff it out (Isaiah 42:3). The Holy Spirit would not leave them. He would restore them. But what about the scores of others who had 'followed' along with the rest, but had never come to faith? Were they not in part a dreadful reflection on us missionaries? We did not minimize our weaknesses and our inadequacies, but even here the Lord had further comfort and encouragement for us, without allowing us to feel complacent.

John 6:60–71 tells us of one of the very great disappointments during our Lord's time on earth. Hundreds, maybe thousands, had been listening to him and 'following' him. As they began to understand the message more clearly, many responded:

'This is a hard saying. Who can accept it?'

John goes on to report that from then on 'many of his disciples turned back and no longer followed him'. We can almost hear the heartache as Jesus turned to the twelve and said:

'You do not want to leave too, do you?'

The example of Paul

The disciple is not greater than his Lord and Paul experienced similar disappointments. He spent two years in Ephesus. God was working there and Luke is able to record that 'all the Jews and Greeks who lived in the province of Asia heard the word of the

Lord' (Acts 19:10). How easy it is to be tempted to envy such a remarkable situation, resulting from God's blessing on the work of the greatest missionary the church has ever known. Yet 'all Asia' cannot have heard from Paul directly. It was as God used the ordinary believers that the word spread throughout the whole of Asia. In a small sense we, too, could say that the whole of the Meligan area had heard the word of the Lord as the Christians had moved around, sharing their faith with anyone who would listen.

No-one doubts that Paul was working 'in the Spirit'. It was the Spirit who had so clearly guided him. His work was not 'wood, hay or straw' (1 Corinthians 3:12). The Lord had called him, worked miracles through him, saved his life, given him many converts. Yet how different the situation in Asia was towards the end of Paul's life. He wrote to Timothy that 'You know that everyone in the province of Asia has deserted me, including Phygelus and Hermogenes' (2 Timothy 1:15). What a pain for him to bear when he was facing the prospect of martyrdom for the sake of the gospel.

In another situation he wrote to the Philippians, 'I hope in the Lord Jesus to send Timothy to you soon... I have no-one else like him... For everyone looks out for his own interests, not those of Jesus Christ' (Philippians 2:19–21). It was at a time when some were preaching Christ 'out of envy and rivalry' (Philippians 1:15).

Real wounds

We are in a battle. We will see great victories but we

must not be deceived into thinking that the enemy will not launch powerful and bitter counter-attacks. The enemy will fight as hard against us as God will allow him to, and sometimes he will appear to be triumphing. If our Lord and Paul experienced set-backs, how can we expect that for us it will be a matter of coasting to victory? We are certainly on the victory side, and we have absolute confidence in the commander-in-chief. But we understand better now that God positively uses set-backs resulting from enemy action to keep us dependent on him, and not on his great blessings, or his strategies to build his church. As the J. B. Phillips translation of James 1:2 puts it: 'When all kinds of trials and temptations crowd into your lives, my brothers, don't resent them as intruders, but welcome them as friends!'

We may be bitterly disappointed, tempted to depression and to give up. Then we need to remind ourselves that only by trusting the Father's choice, the Son's complete victory over Satan on the cross, the power of his resurrection, and the Holy Spirit's working in our lives and the lives of believers, can we survive the disappointments until God allows us to see the maturing fruit.

Purait

Slowly and surely God revitalized his church at Meligan. After many years, the handful of Christians decided that they desperately needed a pastor. Fortunately Purait, a mature, Tagal-speaking Lun Bawang, was willing to go. Purait had had no children. He and his wife had one adopted boy of twelve years. This was an encouragement to the group, as they would be able to support just the three of them, and so it was agreed. Purait was also clearly God's man for the situation. He had much patience and understanding of the struggling church. He prayed, cared deeply, gently drew back the backsliders. He rebuked where necessary and he encouraged. God was using him to rebuild the church. Purait stayed for many years and the Christians were delighted to see their church full once more. Then God moved Purait on. No-one knew quite why at the time, as it left the Meligan church once again without a pastor. We thought perhaps we understood why, in 1984, when we saw God's next step in the re-building programme.

I happened to be sitting with Purait and another long-experienced pastor when the Tagals shared with us at the convention in 1984 (as described in chapter 8). The pastors were finding it quite difficult to see God's hand in the situation. In fact Purait almost seemed grieved that these people, to whom he'd given so many years of his life to nurse them back to faith, were now doing such 'odd' things. He had been a truly faithful servant, and was still caring and praying. He had not lost his zeal for the Lord, but he was not really prepared for God to do unusual things in reviving his church. God understands our limitations and does not force us into situations which we cannot handle. He is continuing to use Purait but he also chose to prepare the Tagal church at Meligan in his own special way for the future.

To think about

Does Jesus have the same sort of problems with us as he did with Peter?

Bookshelf

The Message of 1 Corinthians: Life in the local church, David Prior (IVP, The Bible Speaks Today series, 1985; UK and US editions).
An excellent and very relevant exposition of Paul's letter, written from a burdened heart to a young church with many growing pains.

The Message of Hosea: Love to the Loveless, Derek Kidner (IVP, The Bible Speaks Today series, 1981; UK and US editions).
If we are tempted to give up, it is a great encouragement to remember that God has never given up on us. A commentary on Hosea hardly seems a book that can be read at one sitting, but that is exactly what happened when we lent it to a girl who found it hard to believe that God loved her. 'I can't cope with love like that,' she commented, but was unable to put the book down once she had started reading it.

Spiritual Depression: its causes and cure, D. Martyn Lloyd-Jones (Pickering and Inglis, 1965; now jointly published with STL).
Practical and spiritual help for those who are discouraged. An outstanding book, especially the chapter on 'The Peace of God', in which Dr Lloyd-Jones shows 'the eternal difference between the Christian

way of dealing with anxiety and ... the commonsense way'.

11

Prayer

Prayer is a partnership. God could, of course, do everything so easily without us, but he invites us to share with him in his work. He wants to share his plans with us, and wants us to share our thoughts, hopes, desires and sorrows with him. He wants us to listen to him, and wants to listen to us.

'Peter is going to get converted,' a young soldier, who had become a Christian the previous year, announced one day in Malaya.

'How do you know?'

'He was the first person I witnessed to when I became a Christian. I've been praying on and off for him. Now that I've just had some days in hospital, I've been praying constantly for him. God has now told me that he is going to become a Christian and I must stop praying and start giving thanks.' Peter did get converted very shortly after that.

Listening to God

We don't always hear God speaking to us as clearly as

157

that, partly because God wants us to learn to walk by faith and not by 'sight'. Often God will, for that very reason, speak more explicitly to young Christians. As we grow in the Christian life, and learn to walk by faith, we may not hear so clearly, but often we don't hear because we are not listening. There are also certain dangers when we do try to listen.

I was trying to comfort a distraught missionary who had returned home after just one term's service.

'I was given a prophecy that I was going to marry Mark,' she sobbed. 'When I arrived on the field, I discovered he had just got engaged to someone else.'

It took her a long time to recover from this bitter disappointment. God will speak directly sometimes, but prophecy must always be weighed carefully. We need to be very aware of his voice being confused with our own thinking. That should not, however, stop us from listening.

God always listens to us. As he responds to our prayers, he sometimes changes situations. Sometimes he even appears to have waited to act until we have prayed. At other times he will change us as we pray to bring us into line with his will, and make it appropriate for him to act without being inconsistent. This is a thought Bill first discovered when he was reading C. J. Finney's *Revivals of Religion*, and one which we have quoted and thought about time and again in Borneo, and on numerous occasions since:

'Prayer is that which causes such a change in us as renders it consistent for God to do what was previously not consistent for him to do.'

The same insight is expressed by James Thomson in *The Praying Christ*:

'The aim of prayer is not to make God change his will but to enable us to change our mind and disposition, and thus allow him to do for us and through us what he cannot do until we are fully yielded to him.'

Being open to God

For many years the work of the Mission in Borneo revolved around the 7 a.m. prayer meeting at Lawas. Each of us had to take our turn at leading and sharing something the Lord had been showing us from his Word in recent weeks. It was no good raking up something from years ago. Your fellow missionaries would see through that – and start praying for you to be more open to the Lord as he sought to speak to you personally through his Word. It kept us on our toes. It also meant that we all had to remain alert to what the Lord was saying to us and what he wanted us to pray about.

The prayer meeting seemed to go in cycles as we became aware of God's initiative in leading us to pray about certain things at certain times. The Lord wanted to do these things, but he also wanted us to have a share with him in the partnership of prayer. Some days we would be led to pray for the flying programme specifically or lay leadership training or translation. At other times the burden would be the children in the hostel and the missionaries looking after them. Then there would be a burden for pastors, particularly those in lonely places or those being tempted to give up. There would be the occasions for thanksgiving for answered prayer as one and another returned to Lawas and reported on what the Lord had done in these various areas.

Prayer was so often so specifically answered.

Time and again, we were burdened to pray for the Iban, the largest of the tribes, and yet the one where least seemed to be happening. Day after day we prayed and there seemed to be no encouragement. Here we had to hold on in faith, believing that God had given us the burden. It was many years before God began showing us how he was going to answer those prayers. Yes, it had been a burden he had given us because he knew he was going to call out a church amongst the Iban.

Sometimes days or weeks would go by when the prayer was for the everyday work rather than any special burden. Then the burden would switch to the missionaries and sometimes, only sometimes, to our financial needs.

Our daily bread

Because missionaries' allowances were somewhat low on the list of priorities in the allocation of whatever gifts arrived each month, we were kept aware that the faith of the 'Mission' was the collective faith of all of us as individuals. We couldn't sit back and expect 'them' to pray for the funds to keep the programme going. We had to pray that God would supply our personal needs as well as those of the Mission. We were 'the Mission'. Some of our most exciting experiences of answered prayer came in the realm of the exact provision for a particular need at exactly the right time. And that of course not only encouraged our faith in praying in detail for material things, but in praying for the many spiritual needs too.

We learnt to pray specifically, not just vague, well-phrased prayers. After we'd been home sometime, we realized that that was not always the norm. It seemed that some Christians had not had the privilege of exposure to such specific praying and specific answers.

'Don't be silly. You can't really pray about things like *that*,' a young friend said to us one day when we had been encouraging her to pray that she would find a suitable second-hand car within her price range.

'Of course you can,' we replied. 'We do it all the time in Borneo. God has said that he's numbered the hairs on our heads. Don't you think he is interested in your need for mobility?'

'Well, I suppose so – but why should I expect him to provide me with a car out of the blue – you've been missionaries too long!'

'We're not suggesting that it will be out of the blue, though sometimes it does seem like that. Of course you do all you can to find one. You also commit it to the Lord and believe that he can and will answer in some way or other.'

I went on to tell her about a coat I had wanted to buy. It was in the sale at half-price and the only one of its kind. It seemed a marvellous bargain. But I wasn't sure that I really needed a new coat.

'I left the coat in the shop,' I explained. 'Then I asked the Lord to keep it for me until the next day if he wanted me to have it.'

'That wasn't much of a test of faith, was it?' she queried. 'The shop wasn't open during the night.'

'It was Friday, about 3.30 p.m. when I left the shop. I waited for the hundreds of Saturday morning sale shoppers to snap up this very attractive bargain. At 11 a.m. I phoned. It was still there so I went and bought it. I always said a little prayer of thanks after that when I wore it.'

'I still think you shouldn't bother God with things like that,' our friend protested. 'Anyway, what would you have done if the coat had gone?'

'I'd have accepted the fact that God didn't want me to have it,' I replied.

'That's a good bit of rationalization,' she commented, unimpressed by what I thought was a rather exciting story!

Maybe we don't always need to pray about such details but we are on the whole not specific enough in our praying. We therefore don't have to exercise much faith for a specific answer. It has been wisely said:

'If you aim at nothing, you will sure hit it.'

Being specific in prayer

When we first went to Meligan for a two-month visit to start learning the language, we felt we very much wanted to pray for some real spiritual fruit. We wanted to pray realistically for the people of Meligan. Many of them seemed to be riding on the faith of others in the family. We wanted to see more individuals truly born again. Our faith was not very strong to believe that God could use us in such a short time and with virtually no language. In the end we decided to pray for one deep, lasting conversion. One man and his family (God answered above our asking) came to repentance and to this day they are all standing firm. Even when many fell away, they remained faithful. How we regretted not having had enough faith to pray for more!

Another great advantage of being specific in prayer is the encouragement to our faith when we see God answering.

'Pray where you are,' is an expression we have learnt from a travelling secretary to the universities' Christian Unions. It describes the prayer which is within the limits of our faith.

'If you don't have faith to pray for someone's conversion,' she used to explain, 'then don't. Pray where you are. For example, you can pray for an opportunity to have coffee with the person you are concerned for. God answers that prayer. You may be amazed but your faith is strengthened to ask for the next step. Gradually a friendship develops and you see God answering each progressive prayer. Eventually you will get to the point where you feel you should ask for an opportunity to witness naturally in the course of the conversation.'

That's the point at which we may have a struggle. We may even let the opportunity slip although we are sure God gave it to us as an answer to prayer. We then repent and try again. At last we will be able to pray for the friend's conversion.

By this time it will be in faith, encouraged by the way in which God has answered our prayers as we've moved along in a developing partnership with the Lord. It will also mean we have had an opportunity to build up a friendship. As one Japanese girl put it about a friend she had made while in England:

'My friend built a bridge of friendship and Jesus came walking over it to me.'

Having to wait

God is so ready to answer prayers like this but he does not always do so immediately. We need to be very grateful for this for several reasons. Firstly, if we always had answers to our specific prayers immediately, there is no doubt that we would fall readily to the temptation to a sort of mechanical 'penny-in-the-slot' mentality. I prayed. God answered. It's simple.

Dr Martyn Lloyd-Jones comments on this in his book *From Fear to Faith*: 'If God were unkind enough to answer some of our prayers at once and in our way, we should be very impoverished Christians.'

Thankfully, God knows us through and through. He knows when we need to wait while he convicts us of wrong motives, selfishness or pride or while he leads us into a truer and deeper dependence on him. He knows how much he has to change us or in some way prepare us for his answer.

There is another area of danger when we see God answering prayer quickly and specifically. We come to think that if we don't pray things won't happen.

'If only we'd prayed more, so-and-so would have recovered' is a statement we have heard too often. Whilst recognizing the instructions to 'pray without ceasing' and the lessons to learn from the parable of the importunate widow (Luke 18), a statement like this is inappropriate and can cause untold misery.

The husband of a close friend died a few years ago. He was seventy and very ready to go to be with the Lord. He was in a lot of pain.

'I almost feel like a murderer,' his wife said to us just three weeks before he died. 'Much as I long for him to be healed, I am beginning to pray that the

Lord will take him quickly. He is in so much pain. I can't bear to see it. He wants to go to be with Jesus. We all have to die sometime. I feel, though, that some of my friends are blaming me for no longer joining them in prayer for his healing.'

After her husband's death, it was she who had to comfort the friends in their distress at a time when she quite rightly could have expected them to comfort her.

It is a great relief to know that God takes responsibility in this partnership for answering our prayers with a 'yes', 'no', or 'wait' or by changing us to be in line with his will. It means that we can pray, and pray earnestly, for things before we actually know whether they are in accordance with God's will.

Answers we don't want

I was urgently praying for something on one occasion. I believed it could well be God's will but was not sure. I certainly felt it would be very helpful for someone we cared for. I had prayed and fasted. I began to think that God might be going to say 'no' but the more I thought that the more urgently I prayed. Finally the exact opposite of what I wanted, happened. I was shaken. Had I been selfish and sinning even to have prayed? And was it perhaps my fault therefore that God had not answered my prayer? I was confused. It was then that God drew my attention to the story of David praying for the baby born as the result of his adultery with Bathsheba (2 Samuel 12).

David has sinned. Nathan the prophet comes to him and tells him God's judgment. David repents and God forgives him. Nevertheless Nathan explains that God has said the baby will die.

David puts on sackcloth, refuses to eat and pleads with God for the baby's life. After seven days the baby dies and the servants are afraid that he will do something terrible to himself if they tell him. David guesses. He then astonishes the servants by getting up, washing, worshipping God and having something to eat. They ask for an explantion.

'While the child was still alive, I fasted and wept. I thought, who knows? The Lord may be gracious to me and let the child live. But now that he is dead why should I fast? Can I bring him back again?'

David was praying in actual opposition to the revealed will of God on the grounds that he knew that God was merciful. There is not even a hint in the story that God was in any way displeased with David's praying. Rather it is one of those occasions of two-way communication when God allowed David to express his grief and his hopes – maybe even his anger – while drawing him closer to himself and preparing him for the future. Certainly David changed and in the end worshipped the God who, in his merciful judgment, had caused his grief. God then gave to David another son and this time we read that 'the Lord loved him'.

Arguing with God

Scripture draws a veil over what David actually said to God or what God was saying to David during those seven days. It does however allow us to see another of God's servants battling in prayer with the character of our holy and righteous God.

Several times in Borneo (and since) we have stood with Abraham and said to God:

'You can't do it, Lord!' ('Far be it from you to do such a thing' – Genesis 18:25).

Abraham was battling in Genesis 18 with God's revelation that he was going to destroy Sodom and Gomorrah. He had been learning to trust God ever since he had left Ur of the Chaldees. God had shown himself to be trustworthy. He had rescued Abraham from a number of dangerous situations. He had been utterly reliable. Then suddenly he was saying something which Abraham could not understand at all. This God who enabled him to save the king and people of Sodom from their enemies was now saying that he was about to destroy them utterly.

'Will you sweep away the righteous with the wicked?' Abraham pleads. 'What if there are fifty righteous people in the city? Will you really sweep it away and not spare the place for the sake of fifty righteous people in it? Far be it from you to do such a thing... Far be it from you.'

'If I find fifty righteous people in the city of Sodom, I will spare the whole place for their sake.'

Abraham was encouraged to continue his pleading...forty-five...forty...thirty...twenty, while becoming increasingly aware of the audacity of his questioning. Finally he came to ten.

'May the LORD not be angry, but let me speak just once more. What if only ten can be found there?'

And God said that he would not destroy the city if he found ten righteous in it.

We do not know why Abraham stopped at ten but it must have been that he was satisfied. He was prepared to leave the situation with God. He didn't understand, but once again he could trust God. I

167

can remember the enormous relief and joy of first discovering his wonderful cry of faith, to which we have clung on many an occasion:

'Will not the Judge of all the earth do right?' (Genesis 18:25).

When we can't understand, we can trust the God who has so frequently shown himself to be totally trustworthy.

Prayer as partnership

It is so necessary that God leads us into such struggles in our partnership with him in prayer. We come to a new realization that we do not have 'God in our pockets'. He is so much bigger than a heavenly grandfather, and prayer therefore becomes more real, more of a partnership rather than just asking for things. We come to God *as he is*.

'If we close our minds to everything about God that makes us uncomfortable, we are going through empty motions when we pray. We pray to a god we have ourselves fashioned for our comfort and not to God as he is. True prayer is to respond to the true God as he reveals more of himself by his Spirit in his word. Prayer defined in such terms can be a terrifying experience' (*People in Prayer*, John White, IVP 1977).

We have to come at some time or another to the God of righteous judgment as well as to the God of love. Of course we do not fully understand him. If we could, he would no longer be God. We tell him our dilemma and then have to trust that he is all that he says he is – he is both just and merciful, both holy and loving, both exercising judgment and forgiving the sinner. He is the Judge, who will do right. He may cause or allow suffering, as he did in the days of Habakkuk the prophet. With Habakkuk we can come to a place of acceptance and joy only as we share in this partnership in prayer.

Habakkuk changed his attitude dramatically as he came face to face with God in prayer. His prophecy is a book to which we have turned many a time, both in Borneo and since coming home.

I first became really indebted to Habakkuk when Bill was on his way home from Malaya. Dr Lloyd-Jones was preaching a series of sermons on this prophet's message to us all as the Korean war was shaking the Western world. It has a message to help us face world events, and I needed very much to hear it. It also had a very personal message for me at the time, and has had many times since.

Habakkuk's message to us

Bill was making a three-month detour via Australia on his way home. He had persuaded the Medical Department to transfer a first-class ticket which they had given him to return to England to the shorter but relatively more expensive route to Australia. He then worked his passage from Australia to England as a ship's doctor on a cargo boat. He was paid a nominal sum of one shilling a month and given his board and passage free. It took seven weeks and he had already had several weeks in Australia. This was at the point when I was getting impatient to know whether the Lord was leading us to get married, or whether he was going to take me up on my offer to go to Borneo single.

I prayed and prayed round in circles – the more I prayed the more churned up I became. In fact prayer was becoming an excuse for worry rather than an antedote to it. This was where Dr Lloyd-Jones' exposition of the prophecy helped so much.

Habakkuk has been complaining to God that he is not answering his prayer. God gives him the devastating answer that he is going to raise up the Babylonians to bring judgment on Israel. Habakkuk wisely reminds himself of all he knows about God and confidently affirms that he knows God will not allow his own people to perish. But he is left with a deep problem.

'Your eyes are too pure to look on evil; you cannot tolerate wrong. Why then do you tolerate the treacherous? Why are you silent while the wicked swallow up those more righteous than themselves?' he pleads (Habakkuk 1:13).

He has somewhat missed the point. He has not realized that the wickedness of the privileged people of God was more abhorrent to God than the treachery and wickedness of the Babylonians. Because of this he cannot reconcile the purity of God with his using an ungodly and cruel instrument to bring about his judgment on his chosen people.

After telling God about his perplexity, the prophet shows us how we should handle our bewilderment in prayer. He pictures himself in a watchtower, high above the plain. Dr Lloyd-Jones pointed out that first of all 'we must detach ourselves from the problem...once we have taken a problem to God we should cease to concern ourselves with it. We should turn our backs upon it and centre our gaze on God...But what so frequently happens is this. We go on our knees and tell God about the thing that is worrying us; we tell him that we cannot solve the difficulty ourselves...and we ask him to deal with it and to show us his way. Then the moment we get up from our knees we begin to worry about the problem again...If you take your problem to God, leave it with God. You have no right to brood over it any longer.'

That was what I was doing. I decided I should do what Habakkuk did. The man in the watch-tower is not only above the crowds. He is there to watch. We must not be passive when we have prayed, but we must look for and expect the answer as eagerly as the watchman is looking at the horizon to see the very slightest indication of someone approaching.

Habakkuk continues to communicate with God in prayer, and we see something of the profound change which takes place in him by the time we reach chapter 3. He's heard what God has said concerning the judgment of Israel, and also about the ultimate punishment of their enemies. He has grasped the need for him to live by faith because God is totally reliable. He is now no longer complaining. He's met with God, and throws himself on God's mercy.

'Lord, I have heard of your fame; I stand in awe of your deeds, O Lord. Renew them in our day, in our time make them known; in wrath remember mercy' (Habakkuk 3:2).

He does not fully understand what God is doing, and is fearful. Nevertheless, he has come to see that he can trust God.

'Though the fig-tree does not bud and there are no grapes on the vines, though the olive crop fails and the fields produce no food, though there are no sheep in the pen and no cattle in the stalls, yet I will

171

rejoice in the LORD, I will be joyful in God my Saviour' (Habakkuk 3:17–18).

Habakkuk could see all that was dear to him being swept away. Great suffering lay ahead. Yet he was able to face it because his relationship with God had been established in prayer. God had spoken to him, revealed himself to him, changed his attitudes – all in the two-way communication of prayer.

It seems presumptuous to compare ourselves in any way to Habakkuk. But God invites each one of us to meet with him in this relationship and partnership in prayer. It is one of the greatest privileges and responsibilities which he gives to his children.

To think about

How am I using my privilege of a partnership with God?

Bookshelf

From Fear to Faith, D. Martyn Lloyd-Jones (IVP, 1953).
A classic little book, enabling us to move with Habakkuk from fear and anxiety, through meeting with God in prayer, to a position of trust even in the most severe suffering.

People in Prayer, John White (IVP, 1978; US edition IVP/USA, 1977).
Instead of telling us *how* to pray, the author helps us, as it were, to eavesdrop on the prayers of a number of biblical characters, including our Lord himself. It

is a challenging and moving book, showing great insight into the character of God, and opening up new vistas in prayer.

Mountain Rain, Eileen Crossman (OMF Books, 1982; now jointly published with STL).

Eileen Crossman has written an updated biography of her father, J. O. Fraser, who was a great man of prayer. Using many quotes from his letters, she helps us to see the struggles through which Fraser went as he had to change some of his thinking on prayer. Fraser presents us with a challenge to pray for the church overseas. 'I really believe that if every particle of prayer put up by the home churches on behalf of the infant churches of the mission field were removed, the latter would be swamped by an incoming flood of the powers of darkness...Why prayer is so indispensable we cannot just say, but we had better recognise the fact even if we cannot explain it.'

12

Don't waste suffering

Ruth ● *A shock* ● *Peace* ● *Asking why* ● *Signs and miracles* ● *Return and more separations* ● *A suffering God*

'Why, oh why, Lord?'

We've all said it at one time or another. It is a natural response to suffering.

'If God is a God of love, why does he allow pain, suffering, bereavement?'

That agonized cry of 'Why?' usually develops along two quite different lines over longer or shorter periods.

Either we move slowly towards a confidence in the overall sovereignty and grace of God, even though we do not understand. Or we allow a tiny seed of bitterness to creep in. 'Why, Lord?' becomes 'It's not fair, Lord!' which in turn becomes 'You are not fair, Lord. You don't love me if you allow this to happen to me.' If we allow such feelings to persist, they open the door to a deep-seated resentment, cramping our lives and putting up a barrier between us and God. We blame God for not stepping in to prevent our suffering, little realizing that he has probably done just that a thousand and one times that we knew nothing about. We also lose out on the opportunity to see God providing 'the way of escape, that you may be able to endure it' (1 Corinthians 10:13, RSV).

Ruth

'Be Scots with your suffering. Don't waste a penny of it' was the good advice we heard from a speaker at a convention (which was taking place near the Scottish border). We had left our little handicapped daughter Ruth with some friends for a week while we acted as house-parents to a camp of students attending the convention. Yes, we could endorse that statement as we looked back over several years of battling with this first major suffering in our lives.

Before Ruth, our first baby, was born we had prayed for her, as no doubt almost all young couples do. We prayed that she would be whole – physically, mentally and spiritually. We were on our knees together by our bedside way up in the interior of Borneo. We were excited but awed by the responsibility of bringing up a child – a doubly difficult task for a rather mobile missionary couple. As we finished praying, we stayed on our knees and looked at each other. We were both experiencing a strange sense of un-ease.

'Do you think we really should have prayed like that? Isn't it rather inappropriate?' One of us voiced the feelings of both. The baby was the gift of the giver of 'every good and perfect gift' (James 1:17). Should we not trust him? For the first and only time in our lives, we felt God clearly leading us to withdraw our prayer. We talked it over, specifically withdrew the prayer and prayed again:

'Father, please glorify your name in this little life and in ours too. The rest we leave with you.'

We firmly believed then (though without knowing why), and have done ever since, that God directed that prayer. When our next two children were on the way, the Lord gave us perfect liberty to pray that they would be sound in body, mind and spirit.

As we look back, we realize that God was bringing us into partnership with him. When we were praying, God already knew the baby was going to be handicapped. He also knew that he was going to bring great glory to his name through her. In a way unique in our experience he led us to come onto his wavelength even though we didn't know the significance of it at the time.

Ruth was born in Bill's own teaching hospital during our first leave in England. She appeared to be perfect, not just to the biased parents! It was months before there was even the slightest suspicion that anything might be not quite right. In fact we were on our way back to Borneo after a very busy six months of leave. We had noticed that she clenched her left hand and we had often dangled a toy over it to encourage her to open it. But she was strong, sat bolt upright quite early, and seemed in every other way normal.

We'd been back for several months working at our headquarters when the time came for us to return to Tagal country. Ruth was nearly twelve months and in so many ways seemed such a totally normal, healthy, attractive little girl. But Bill was getting seriously concerned and did not want to carry this burden alone, medically, particularly not for some months in the rather inaccessible village of Meligan.

'I think we need a second opinion,' he said one day. 'I don't think as a father I can be objective enough. We need to know whether there is anything we should be doing.' He was speaking very guardedly so as not to worry me. He was also up to his eyes in work that needed to be done before setting off for the interior. We decided I should take Ruth for a consultation. There were always heavy demands for a seat on the little single-engined aircraft wherever it was flying, and it didn't seem right to take up two and a half places when one and a half would do. Bill gave me a letter to take to the doctor.

A shock

The Shell Oilfields Company was always very generous to the missionary personnel, and one of their highly qualified staff was willing to see Ruth. We chatted and he started to examine her. Disarmed by her attractiveness and charm he suggested that she might have a bit of a 'club' foot. But then he went silent, and continued to do some tests. He tested her left foot time and time again. At last he said:

'I can't believe it. I have to tell you, your daughter is spastic.'

'Spastic!' I exclaimed, as my mouth went dry and my legs seemed to buckle.

'Yes,' he replied, but seeing the colour drain from my face, he went on, 'Don't worry. It's exceedingly mild. She's a strong, bright little thing. By the time she's eight or so she'll have fully compensated for any handicap.' And he started to explain that other parts of the brain would take over the functions of the damaged brain cells. We would need to do exercises with her, but we did not have a lot to worry about.

As with everyone else we consulted over the next few years, Ruth's attractiveness and bright personality deceived him, but we were not to know that for several years. Maybe God knew that we couldn't take it at the time. The doctor's explanation certainly sounded feasible. It helped me over my initial shock, but how I wished that Bill had been able to come with me. Nevertheless, during the hour's flight back to Lawas, I experienced an extraordinary calm.

The rest of the day was full of activity and preparation, and we set off for Meligan the following day. There was great excitement as we landed on the tiny airstrip. Everyone crowded around to welcome us and to see Ruth. They stroked her blonde hair and her little white arms. The majority of them had never seen a white baby before. They were so loving and so pleased to see us. We hardly had time to think.

Then it hit us! Spastic! We crumpled. We wanted only to cry and cry and cry. We wanted to run off into the jungle so that we didn't have to see anyone or talk to anyone.

'Why, Lord? Spastic! She doesn't look spastic. Could it be wrong?'

'We're missionaries, Lord. We can't cope with a spastic daughter in this situation.'

'We've sacrificed everything for you, Lord. Why have you allowed this to happen to us?'

The questions, the arguments, the tears, went on for three days. A glimmer of hope came as we thought back to all the confirming signs that the Lord had so graciously given us when we had got engaged.

'Is this why you wanted us to be so sure that it was you who had brought us to marriage, Lord? Lord, you have got us into this situation. You will have to see us through.'

Bill kept seeing long queues of sick people in between sessions on the language. I tried to do some language analysis work and look after Ruth but my concentration was almost nil. We resented having to talk to our Tagal friends. How could they understand our heartache when Ruth looked so fit and well compared with their sick little babies and children? We felt isolated from them. During those three days we seemed like robot missionaries. We couldn't pray, and we certainly couldn't love and care for those around us.

'Lord, we'll have to go home if you don't do *something*! We are useless as missionaries. In fact we are doing more harm than good if we go on like this.'

Peace

Light began to dawn as the Lord reminded us of the way in which he had led us to pray for Ruth before she was born. This little girl was going to glorify the Lord. We didn't know how but we could hold on to that. The Lord loved us and he loved Ruth. He was in control. And then something really wonderful happened. The Lord filled both our hearts to overflowing with his peace. We have often said that it was as if he gave us peace on a plate. It was not only incredible; it was overwhelming. 'The peace of God, which *transcends all understanding*,' (it certainly did that) 'will guard [garrison] your hearts...' (yes, it was like a wall around us) (Philippians 4:7). In his love and his power, he was going to help us to cope. We knew that he alone could reconcile the calling of being missionaries with the problem of a handicapped child. He had given Ruth to us. He was the giver of every good and perfect gift. We could trust him and our hearts were warmed.

Perhaps if we had known the tears, the stress, the heartache and the physical tiredness that were to come, we might have pushed away the peace as being too unrealistic. But we didn't, and stage by stage, God helped us through. Although the peace was assailed, it stayed with us over the years. We never lost the assurance that Ruth was God's love gift to us, that he was in control and that he would see us through. But he did more. Through Ruth, he made us into people with more understanding of those less fortunate than ourselves. In a very special way, he used her to bring glory to his name, both in us and in a number of other people. There was so much that she taught us all.

I was translating John's Gospel when the little five-year-old daughter of two of our fellow missionaries died of a brain tumour. We, as a mission team, were very much a family in those days and when one member suffered, we all suffered. A colleague came to visit us one morning.

'Won't it be wonderful for Jenny [the little girl's mother] when she gets to heaven and can ask God why he should have taken little Linda!' she commented. And then she added:

'And it will be great for you too to ask why God allowed Ruth to be handicapped.'

Asking why

I agreed whole-heartedly and we chatted for a few minutes. My friend left and I returned to the task of preparing John 16 for translation the next day. I was still thinking of Ruth and Linda.

'In that day you will ask nothing of me... Ask, and

you will receive, that your joy may be full' (John 16:23–24, RSV).

I noticed that the word 'ask' in the Malay New Testament was translated by two different words. Of course that had to be investigated. The commentaries pointed out the use of the two different words for 'ask', but the explanations left the choice for translation somewhat open. I then turned to J. B. Phillips. He had translated the first part of the verse, 'on that day you will not ask me any questions'. He had then actually started a new paragraph in the middle of the verse. The new paragraph dealt with the other sort of asking in order to receive something. That was exactly the differentiation which the Malay had made.

I stopped translation preparation and thought about it. Of course my mind went back to Ruth and Linda. It seemed to me that God was saying in these verses that, when we see the Lord face to face, we will not need to ask him 'why?' We will then *know* that everything that has happened to us has been under the overall control of his love; that he has allowed sadness and evil limited access only to our lives; that he has been weaving 'all things...together for good to them that love God' (Romans 8:28, AV).

If that is so when we see the Lord, might it not be possible so to love him and to trust him that we can know, here and now, that everything that happens to us is turned to our good by our wise, loving, omnipotent Father? Then we can say with Job, 'The LORD gave and the LORD has taken away; may the name of the LORD be praised' (Job 1:21).

This is not to say there will not be tears and questionings. But they will lead us on slowly to a deeper faith rather than opening the door for an insidious bitterness to creep in.

Was this something we learnt once and for all? Sadly not. We had to learn to trust God afresh in each situation, but at least we had the confidence of knowing he had helped us in one big situation already and this encouraged our weak faith.

Signs and miracles

Any married missionary couple with children has to face a very major sacrifice when children come to school age. Education of children almost inevitably means separations. We were home for two years battling over whether God's plan for us was to leave Ruth in England. We eventually concluded it was. Thankfully, God knew of the cost that such a decision would cause. He therefore graciously confirmed our guidance with a series of signs and miracles.

Bill was doing a General Practitioner's locum in Reading. He had been called to see a patient, who happened to be the pastor of a Baptist church.

'You can't possibly preach on Sunday,' Bill said to him after examination.

'I must. There is no-one else.'

'It's just not on with a throat like that,' Bill insisted.

'Then you'll have to do it for me,' the pastor rejoined, knowing that Bill was not unused to preaching.

Bill took both the services. Joan Morris, the wife of a leading member of the church was present, and the next day she was visiting the pastor. His wife had recently died and Joan had been doing his washing for him.

'What a pity those two can't go back to Borneo,' he commented to her during conversation. 'They are so much needed there,' he added.

'Oh, can't they?' Joan replied. 'Why not?'

'Well,' the pastor said, 'they have a little spastic daughter, and they can't take her back with them.'

Joan thought no more of it for several weeks. Then, quite unexpectedly, the Lord spoke to her during a missionary Sunday in the church. She has no recollection who the speaker was, but during the service, it was as if the Lord was persistently saying to her:

'You offer to look after that little spastic girl, so that her parents can go back to Borneo.'

'Oh, no, Lord,' she protested. 'I'm far too busy in the church. Anyway I've never heard of the BEM and I don't know the Lees. It's not as if they were in a mission I'm praying for.'

But the feeling remained that God was telling her to look after Ruth. She couldn't get away from it.

'Oh, all right, Lord,' she prayed. 'If you want me to, then bring me into contact with Dr Lees to-morrow.' She was not in the habit of throwing out challenges like this to the Lord. In fact it was most uncharacteristic of her. But it gave her peace.

She went to visit the pastor the next day, calm in the thought that his throat was better. What she did not know was that his son had been taken ill. She had not been there long when there was a ring at the doorbell. She opened the door. It was Bill. She said nothing but went home to share the events with her husband and four children.

Joan wrote to us and eventually we arranged for her to come to see us after the children's bed-time. Ruth heard voices and came trotting downstairs to

183

see what was happening. She climbed onto Joan's lap as if she had known her all her life.

Ruth didn't look spastic – just a normal little girl. Joan would have had her whatever she had looked like, but this was a lovely joy for her. Added to that her name was Ruth, Joan's favourite name and the one they were going to give to their second daughter, if they had had one. They then had three boys!

'I've got my Ruth at last,' Joan said later, delighted in yet another of the tiny little signs God gave. There were so many that they added up to strong confirmation of the leading that God had been giving us all.

In fact there were miracles upon miracles! How gracious God was to give us so many signs that he wanted us to do something which we so much did not want to do. Within a couple of months we were on our way back to Borneo and to four years of separation. Four years of seeing God helping Jack and Joan as they looked after Ruth. Four years of getting on with the job of translating and building up the Tagal church. But it was not going to be easy for any of us.

Return and more separations

Ruth had had measles encephalitis shortly before our return, and although she had obviously recovered from it, we noticed some considerable changes. Joan kept us well in touch and we shared with her the agony of further changes. Ruth began to lose her balance after a series of epileptic fits. Then her talking got less and less until she had just two words – 'Amen' and 'Thank-you'! Sometimes we wondered whether we should come home. Often we worried about Joan. She had deliberately not told us previously that she had had slight heart trouble and the doctor had told her that having Ruth might shorten her life. But constantly we were reminded that it was the Lord who had called Joan and who was enabling her. Just as the Tagal New Testament was finished, we readily responded to an SOS for us to fly home instead of coming by boat, because Ruth had deteriorated considerably in the previous few weeks.

Ruth came back into our home with incredibly little trauma, thanks to the way in which Joan had kept the memory of us alive for her. But she continued to deteriorate. She finally went to be with the Lord at the age of fourteen, bringing glory to the Lord in her death as in her life.

It was not only through our handicapped daughter that we experienced the pain of separation. Our second daughter, Heather, was six when we went back to Borneo, leaving Ruth in England. She was excited to be going back and to be joining all her old friends. They were on holiday when we arrived but soon she would be joining them at the hostel in Kota Kinabalu. The children lived at the hostel with one of our missionary couples as 'parents' and attended school in the area. She couldn't wait to get there. In the days before she left, she'd packed and re-packed her case beautifully neatly several times.

The day for departure came. She smilingly boarded the little aircraft and was away, not at all realizing how long fourteen weeks would be, although we had tried to prepare her realistically. We knew only too well that there was little prospect of seeing her during that time, but I kept saying to myself, 'If she's happy, then I too can be happy.'

Each week the children wrote to their parents in various parts of Borneo. Almost every week Heather's opening sentences were, 'How are you? I am fine', but this soon began to sound a little hollow as we began to suspect that she was not settling. She came home for Christmas. She was not fine. We told ourselves she would settle down in time. The other children had done. We plodded on term after term. Frequently on the surface all was well but for various reasons she was not settling as well as some of the others. We eventually sent an SOS prayer letter home to a few friends.

'Please pray for Heather,' we asked, 'and pray especially that she will not be bitter when she grows up, because we were missionaries.' That was all. Of course we were praying daily too.

We thought the situation might ease when Val, her young sister, joined her after three years. Whether it was merely that she could express herself better in letters or whether it was because of her deep concern for Val, we don't know, but we had comments like this:

'Dear Mummy and Daddy,

How are you? Val and I are fine but we cry a lot.'

I remember walking up and down the grass airstrip which ran through the middle of our headquarters. I told God I hated every blade of grass in Borneo. And I hated him for calling me to be there and causing my little daughters to suffer.

Of course as soon as I'd verbalized that, I knew it was an outrageous sin. I told the Lord how sorry and miserable I felt to have even thought it and asked for his forgiveness. God not only forgave me but he filled my heart with an overwhelming sense of his love, his forgiveness and his presence. I still longed to return home, but God knew all about my situation and he loved us all. He was caring for Ruth at home. She was happy. He would care for Heather and Val in Borneo. And he would help us all not to 'waste' this particular suffering.

A suffering God

He did it in two ways. We hope not irreverently in any way comparing ourselves to God, but we felt that we were having the merest glimmer of an insight into how much God must have suffered to see his Son suffering while on earth. We think a lot, and rightly so, about the sufferings of Christ. Do we ever stop to meditate on how greatly the Father also suffered through his plan of salvation? Any experience, however painful, which opens our minds and hearts to a greater appreciation of the depth of the love of God, has to be one from which we ultimately benefit.

God also gave us the joy of seeing how he was going to draw the girls closer to himself. We arrived home with Heather aged ten and Val aged seven. Both, according to some of our friends, were showing real signs of insecurity. Had we made too many sacrifices on their behalf? Should we have come home sooner and not stopped to get the Tagal New Testament finished? After we had been home twelve months and given the girls the secure home which they so much needed, we had a visit from a friend who had stayed with us in the first month of our being home.

'I've never seen two such transformed children,'

he commented. Then he added, 'I didn't say so at the time, but I was really worried about them when I saw them twelve months ago.'

God had answered prayer, but the girls were still young. Would they yet turn round on us for 'sacrificing' them? When Heather was about fourteen we were talking about the 'hostel' days. I asked her if she could remember being unhappy at times and with a lovely smile she said:

'Oh, Mummy, I can only remember the nice things.'

Maybe an even more significant remark came from Val, when she was a student and facing up to the missionary challenge:

'I'd like to be a missionary because I see all the good that it has done for you and for us. I'd like my children to have the same advantages, but I'm not sure if that's the best sort of motive for being a missionary!'

Our God is certainly a God who answers prayer. He has answered ours for the girls and done 'immeasurably more than all we ask or imagine' (Ephesians 3:20).

We ask again, looking back over our experiences, 'Is it sacrifice?'

To think about

1. Meditate on J. B. Phillips' translation of James 1:2: 'When all kinds of trials and temptations crowd into your lives, my brothers, don't resent them as intruders, but welcome them as friends!'

2. Look for examples in your own life where bad

188

things have turned out to be a blessing (Romans 8:28).

Bookshelf

Why us?: When bad things happen to God's people Warren Wiersbe (IVP, 1984).
A helpful study on the theology of suffering, particularly chapter 4 on Job.

Job (Tyndale Old Testament Commentaries) Francis I. Andersen (IVP, 1976).
One of the best of a very good series of commentaries.

The Enigma of Evil, John Wenham (IVP, 1985).
Formerly published under the title, 'The Goodness of God', this has been one of the most influential books in our lives. It deals so ably and helpfully with the moral questions of the Old Testament in particular and has an excellent chapter on suffering.

The Suffering and the Glory, David Prior (Hodder and Stoughton, 1985).
How we empathize with David Prior when he writes about his preaching on Philippians 3:10 'that I may know him and the power of his resurrection...', but leaving out the last part of the verse 'and may share his sufferings, becoming like him in his death'. We used to do the same but, with him, have come to see that this 'glory minus suffering' message is very inadequate. 'The Suffering and the Glory', based on 2 Corinthians, gives a balanced and biblical perspective on what it means to be a disciple of Christ.

The problem of pain, C.S. Lewis (Fontana, 1957).
C.S. Lewis looks at the problem of how we come to terms with a good and all powerful God who allows pain and suffering.

When the roof caves in, Oswald Sanders (OMF Books, Living Testimony Series, 1985).
Missionaries share their experiences of pain and suffering and how they have survived bereavement, accident, sickness and separations. Oswald Sanders concludes this book with some biblical insights which help us to react in trust rather than bitterness.

Joni, Joni Eareckson with Joe Musser (new edition Pickering and Inglis, 1980; now jointly published with STL).
The well-known story of Joni who, at the age of 17, had a diving accident which left her totally paralysed from the shoulders. We follow her through battles with anger, bitterness, depression and confusion into a life of purpose for God.